HEROIC OWNERSHIP

HEROIC OWNERSHIP

Build Your Team, Plan Your Exit,
Create Your Legacy

D. Scot Hunsaker

**BOOK**LOGIX®
Alpharetta, GA

ISBN: 978-1-61005-938-1

Library of Congress Control Number: 2017916626

10 9 8 7 6 5 4 3 2   1 2 2 9 1 7

Printed in the United States of America

⊗This paper meets the requirements of ANSI/NISO Z39.48-1992 (Permanence of Paper)

CONTENTS

FOREWORD

There are fewer paths more exciting and rewarding than creating your own business and going out on your own. Many try and fail, for many reasons. For many more, it remains a lifelong dream. For a few, it becomes a reality. I am one of those lucky few, and if you're reading this, you probably are too.

If you have established a successful, profitable business that has survived for ten years or more, congratulations! You have beaten the odds. Less than half of new businesses last that long. But if your presence is required to operate the business, you still have important work to do.

To create a legacy, and this is what Scot's excellent book is about, you need to create a business that will be able to sustain itself without you. This is an exceptionally difficult thing to do. It requires more courage, humility, thoughtfulness, and relationship-building than it did to start the business. And it may involve a lot of "unlearning" before you can learn how to do it.

Scot's book is an easy read (I read it in one day), but it delivers a powerful and unforgettable message about the perils, pitfalls, and potential of leadership. With personal stories, humility, generosity, and practical, hard-won wisdom, Scot shares his journey, warts and all. From his father's iron-willed control and a difficult handoff, he was able to create a lasting organization and a team that was ready, when he was, to go into debt and buy the business from him, in cash.

Can you imagine that happening in your business?

Most owners think this is something they can think about later, when they are ready to retire. But for most of us, by then, it will be too late.

You create your legacy every day, by the actions you take and the decisions you make.

If you want your company to live on when your time is done, if you want to walk away with cash for all your hard work, if you want to hand a solid company over to a new generation of leaders, and most importantly, if you want to walk away smiling, happy, and fulfilled—read on.

I promise you this is a book like Scot himself: warm, friendly, personable, and practical. One thing Scot will never do is waste your time, and this book is no exception. It's a joy to read such a concise business book with such clear, actionable takeaways.

Enjoy!

—Dave Gray

Founder of XPLANE

Author of *The Connected Company*,

Gamestorming, and *Liminal Thinking*

ACKNOWLEDGMENTS

Thank you to my parents, Joe and Sandy Hunsaker, for giving me the freedom to learn through trial and error and having the trust to let me spread my wings.

Thank you to my family, Sue, Brooke, and Ben, for supporting me in our journey and taking risks.

Thank you to my coworkers and partners for having the confidence to develop a common vision and executing it.

Thank you to my many mentors who helped coach me and provided the skillset to achieve my goals and objectives.

And thank you to my book team at Bigwidesky for making this book a reality.

INTRODUCTION

YOUR LEGACY IS EVERYTHING

It's hard to see the picture while inside the frame.
—John C. Maxwell

In late 2012, after a twenty-four-year career and thirteen years leading Counsilman-Hunsaker, I sold my company to my employees for cash.

I now look back on that day as one of my proudest moments as a business owner. The transfer itself was nothing terribly special. Like most transactions in business, it was comprised of a series of papers solidified with ink. But represented on that day was something much more than mere words; it was everything we had worked for together. All of our partners from around the country came to our St. Louis location, many with their spouses and children, some of whom sat on their parents' laps while they signed the closing documents. It hit me in a way that I did not expect. I can only describe it as everything we had worked for.

Most business leaders are perfectionists, and I am no exception. It isn't often that I grant myself a moment of self-congratulation. But I felt an enormous sense of pride that day. I felt that I had been a good steward of the company my father had created. It was also a fast ownership transition, taking only forty-five days from proposal to close, an unusually short interval for such a task. To me, that meant that there was a great deal of trust involved. My partners wanted their families there to share the experience. To me, it meant their commitment was deep and earnest, almost like a marriage. I was confident that the group around the table would have courage when they faced the challenges sure to lie ahead.

As leaders, we touch hundreds of lives. It is a tremendous privilege and awesome responsibility. I do not share this story with you to gloat; I want to share with you because I think you, a business owner, can appreciate what this was like in a way most people cannot. We know the risks of creating and molding something. Each day we live in some amount of dread or fear that our vision may fail. That thought sounds something like this: *What if this thing I'm making, which requires all of my time, energy, and resources, fails?* And once your business gets off the ground, the fear of failure doesn't go away. It just evolves into another worry: *If it does succeed, how will I keep it successful?* Perhaps this kind of fear surfaces as a transitory thought or a quick illusion before retreating back into our psyche, where we've trained it to remain so it doesn't disrupt us.

Running a business is an infinite task. It seems to regenerate each time you check one task off the list: managing employees, negotiating client relationships, narrowing down the exact specifics of a project, working with accountants, lawyers, contractors, web developers—to the point where the urgency of daily tasks outweighs your capability to work on the trajectory of your business.

Don't confuse the urgent with the important.

Even in the midst of all that urgent stuff, I can tell you that it also wasn't just by luck or happenstance that everything involved with selling my company clicked together within forty-five days. The successful, fulfilling, and life-changing transfer of ownership was a process years in the making. We were able to have that moment together that day because, long ago, I realized that legacy was everything I did, and that, one day, I would need to create something worth passing on.

My Vision for You

The same is true for you, which is what led me to write this book. History tells us that everything ends. And that means this company that you've toiled over for years will end one day, as well. So, the question for you is simple: what will your end be? Or, perhaps more accurately, are you going to create the legacy or be a victim of circumstance? My vision for you is that you can create something that is sustainable long after you are no longer alive.

We aren't big fans of talking about death in Western civilization. There's no quicker way to kill a conversation. As morbid as it may sound, a lasting legacy depends on how willing we are to grapple with the idea of what will happen to our organization when we are no longer around to run it. A lasting legacy isn't simply something that happens. The success of your legacy depends on how willing you are to develop an action plan that will take the trajectory of your business and shape it for maximum success long after you're gone.

The number-one hope I have for you is that upon reading this book, you take action toward creating the legacy you want. It is also my hope that this book serves as a helpful guide with tools that allow for meaningful progress and the ability to make knowledgeable decisions about how to go forward. I hope you see this book as a set of concepts you can use to think about how to not only make you more successful today, but to continue that success after you are no longer the leader of your company.

How This Book Is Structured

This book is split into two parts. Part I describes the set of principles that make up what legacy is; Part II is about creating your legacy. Both sections are based on my journey and the wisdom I gathered from others. This book is not theory. It is not a series of philosophies. This kind of conceptual thinking was not something that came natural to me. I am not more gifted than any other business owner. The principles and action plan I came upon were born out of my own experiences.

It is understandable that the kinds of ideas and actions I outline in Parts I and II may seem like a tall order. Why plan for tomorrow when there's a mile-high pile of urgent requests on your desk and a thousand emails to address in your inbox today? While putting out fires and managing urgency *within* the business, it's not uncommon for the important work of what ultimately happens *to* the business to get lost in the fray. What do you want your business to look like five, ten, twenty years from now? Thirty years from now? Four generations from now? What if we challenged ourselves to think differently about not only the importance of working *in* the business, but also working *on* the business?

From my vantage point, if you're making something, you're on the journey of what will eventually happen to it, whether that journey is acknowledged and addressed or not. As a serial business owner myself, I can share my personal experience and what has worked for me to ensure the businesses I've led function without needing me every step of the way.

We aren't victims of circumstance. We have choices. In Part I, my goal is to help define those choices about the journey and recognize all the paths that are available. You might as well make knowledgeable decisions about the path you're on to ensure it outlasts you, rather than traveling on the journey of your organization and being subject to its twists and turns without knowing it. I'll be the first to say planning doesn't guarantee the outcome. However, it does allow for a sense of direction over the elements of business trajectory that leaders can control.

The second part of the book is the how. I'll share some of the tools I've learned while traveling down various paths and how they worked in my business. Take what resonates with you, and leave what doesn't.

What I learned through my journey is that legacy is, and always has been, everything. We create our legacy whether we mean to or not, so why not be intentional about it? I do not think this book outlines the only way to get it, but it is the path we took at Counsilman-Hunsaker, and it is the path successful clients and colleagues have taken. I firmly believe as leaders, there's very little we can do that's going to impact today. As leaders, what we're really doing is making decisions that will hopefully have an impact three months, six months, a year, two years, three years, or even three generations down the road to create the kind of legacy we desire.

PART I

CHAPTER 1

DECISIONS CASCADE

Both of my father's parents died when he was young. That meant, from an early age, he had to learn how to take care of himself. He realized that if he wanted to achieve anything, it was up to him. Around the time he was a teenager, most of the celebrity role models he had were self-made men. John Wayne, Marlon Brando, and Humphrey Bogart were strong types who set out to get what they wanted.

That kind of driven man was appealing to Joe, my father. In his St. Louis high school he was an overachiever, winning accolades as an outstanding swimmer. He carried on his athletic competitiveness into a college career at the University of Illinois. Joe was a two-time national champion and world record holder. He won an NCAA championship in the 200-yard individual medley in 1958 as a junior with Illinois before winning a title in the event at the National AAU Championships the following year. In December 1958, Joe set the world record in the 200-meter individual medley at the East West Collegiate Swimming Meet held in Fort Lauderdale, Florida.

After college, my father was a quintessential entrepreneur. He started several successful (and some not-so-successful) ventures.

From the time I was a boy, I witnessed what it was like to be an entrepreneur. It meant working from six a.m. to six p.m. seven days a week. And, for my father, it meant everything he had.

In 1970, he teamed up with swimming legend James "Doc" Counsilman and formed Counsilman-Hunsaker and Associates. They were truly entrepreneurial at the time, setting industry standards for competitive swimming pools and aquatic recreation experiences. Being naturally driven competitors, their business grew quickly. My father fully embraced being at the helm of his enterprise. He did what I call "management by memo." He would have an assistant to whom he would dictate his commands, and others in the company would be expected to execute. He delegated very little of the decision-making. The most central source of value in the company started and stopped with him. It was a horse only he could ride—not a good way to create value.

I wanted you to know this brief history of Joe for a particular reason having to do with a foundational concept of this book: the creation of a lasting legacy. In the consulting work I do today, I am approached by business owners who seem to believe that legacy creation is something to be trifled with in the last couple years of owning a company. This is a mistake. The truth is this: Your legacy begins now, in this moment, *because every decision you make has a cascading effect on the future of your company.* The decisions you make in the present moment set a course for what will happen in the future. And while this may sound like a no-brainer, many intelligent business leaders I know live in a state of denial about this simple truth. They believe that if they keep making money, then the legacy will work itself out. From my experience, those circumstances are extremely rare.

My understanding of this foundational principle of cascading decisions is why I typically begin discussions about creating legacy with a simple question: *what is your definition of success?* Is it wealth? Is it influence? Does it involve the creation of a business that will continue after you're gone?

For me, it was creating a business that would thrive after I was no longer there. I wanted to find emerging leaders, transfer knowledge, and help them to become strong enough to face the uncertainty that comes with ownership. That, for me, was success. I wanted something I could leave to my team and their families.

Clarity regarding your definition of success as a business leader is critical to legacy creation. Because, articulated or not, you have one. It is already affecting the decisions you make. And each of those decisions is creating a cascade that is shaping your legacy—right now.

What is your definition of success?

My definition of success was different from my father's. That is not to say I did not learn a great deal from him; I soaked up more than can be captured in this book. And not because he was one of those helicopter parents who asked for a game of catch every day. In fact, his style at home reflected his style at work. My siblings and I were usually left to our own devices. This allowed me the space to explore and become self-reliant. It also allowed me the time to decide that I did not want to manage or lead the way my father did.

Breaking My Father's Cascade

Based on my father's experiences and his models for leadership, his unarticulated personal mission statement in life was: If you want something done right, you have to do it yourself. This statement was great for driving toward results, but it created little room for emerging leaders within an organization or for sharing knowledge.

Since he was so self-reliant, one of my father's decisions as an owner was that he would never allow partners. Doc Counsilman, the namesake of the business, was not involved in the day-to-day business, though he owned shares. That decision did not just have one short-term outcome. It meant that if big decisions needed to be made, they could only be made by one person. It meant that if a senior person hoped to achieve an ownership stake, then that was not available to them. This resulted in some great people leaving. That, in turn, had an effect on the structures and systems within the company to support the mission.

You can follow this cascade to the moment I assumed leadership of the company. When I bought Counsilman-Hunsaker from him, he prevented me from bringing on partners—at first, anyway. I realized that other people in the organization knew more about certain aspects of aquatics and business, and I felt strongly that unless other people had a real stake in the future outcomes of the company, leadership titles were mere window dressings. Several of my business mentors asked me, "Why would you sell twenty percent of your stock under very favorable terms? You're giving up that income. What's in it for you?" I countered that for the first three to five years, it'd be likely that there would be very little in it for me. At that time, I was taking the bulk of the business risk. It could have been a disaster, but it was my plan to invest in the future leadership of the organization with the hope of creating an all-for-one, one-for-all attitude. We needed each other for the business to work.

When I made the decision to expedite buying my father out of the company and bringing partners into the business, I was making a bigger statement than just the short-term structure change. That decision had the potential to cascade into the kind of future I preferred. While the immediate consequences were a bit painful, it was a present-moment decision that would be in alignment with my definition for legacy success.

What I want you to appreciate, more than anything, is that a definition for success or an end game must be present with decision-making if you hope to achieve that end. Because your legacy is now.

By bringing on partners, I communicated my ultimate intention: to go on this business journey together with my employees. This message had greater clarity in action than anything I could have ever communicated with words. This was a completely new path for the organization. It created a new cascade and new sets of crossroads that allowed us to accomplish amazing things we never could have done individually.

My Personal Mission Statement

Before I ever considered becoming a leader in my father's company, I began developing a personal mission statement. Perhaps it's not unique, but when it comes to leadership my personal strategy has been to find the best possible people, give them the best possible tools, and then get out of the way. Much like my father, this mission statement is a mashup of my experiences and the role models I was provided. But unlike my father, I wanted to focus on creating the kind of place that could identify who had the will and ability to lead the organization—a search that needed to begin the first day I was on the job.

Along with your definition of success or realizing the end you hope to achieve, a personal mission statement helps to make the day-to-day decisions match your vision. In times of uncertainty, when the right decision does not seem clear, a mission statement will guide your behavior. It will make it simpler to stay the course toward the legacy you hope to create.

When you look back on your career, what will make you the most proud?

Conscious Decisions Create a Legacy

All of the decisions we made at Counsilman-Hunsaker shaped me and our organization in ways that had far-reaching effects. Those cascades are still happening within the walls of Counsilman-Hunsaker, though it has been years since I worked there.

Some of you may read this chapter and think, "This is nothing new. I understand there is a cause-and-effect relationship and that those decisions compound." You are correct; it is not new. But few business leaders I have met—in particular the ones who would like to be shaping a legacy—live each day as though this insight were true. Your legacy is shaped by the decisions that you make in this moment. I can show you all of the how-tos, but if you cannot accept this idea and admit to your innermost self your legacy begins now, then the rest of the chapters will not take hold.

In the process of creating a sustainable legacy, I have learned that decisions are the fundamental building blocks of a legacy. Once we understand what decisions really are and how they work, we can become mindful of the kinds of cascades our decisions create.

CHAPTER 2

CASCADES ARE EITHER CREATIVE OR LIMITING

The people who have been most influential in shaping my notions about what legacy means are the ones I met in my formative years. And, like so many of those experiences, it was not until I became older that I grew to appreciate their knowledge. I'm reminded of the adage "Youth is wasted on the young."

Aside from my father, one of the influential people I had the privilege to meet during my youth was Dr. William Haeberle, a business professor I had when I attended Indiana University. Already a successful serial entrepreneur in his own right, Haeberle was able to make even the most mechanical of business concepts come to life with real-world experience. Every year, he would select several student apprentices in the business school to learn about what I like to call the "art of business." Though I did not know it at the time, it was really leadership training on a higher level.

This extra engagement didn't just include time with him where he showered more knowledge upon us. In fact, Haeberle was the least academic person in academia. Instead, we learned by doing and participating in the real world of business. Haeberle would take us to actual company board meetings, where we could see firsthand how he worked with leaders. We saw the interactions he would have with stakeholders at a board meeting or an informal hallway conversation. We heard the questions he used to gain strategic information to make more knowledgeable decisions. He took us to meetings with bankers to teach us how to develop strong working relationships with people who understood finance. We saw how to prepare a business with the intellectual strength needed to take advantage of opportunities.

This man from my youth, Dr. Haeberle, was important in helping to cultivate the next foundational element in building a lasting legacy. In the previous chapter, the focus was on the present-day decisions we make as business leaders. Those decisions have cascading impacts on the future. Dr. Haeberle, however, uncovered for me a deeper understanding and a way to interpret the quality of the cascades we create. Through his example, I began to understand that the decisions we make can either have a limiting or creative impact on the future. That sounds a bit abstract, so let me explain further.

Instead of filling my head with another accounting theory, Haeberle focused me on the ways to navigate and sustain vital business relationships. As a bunch of college-aged men and women, we didn't have a clue how to dress for work, business gatherings, or meetings. He took us to a haberdasher, taught us how to pack for a business trip, and instructed us on how to work a cocktail party or networking event. He told us things that seemed miniscule at the time such as, "Carry your drink in your left hand instead of your right, so your hand isn't wet and clammy when you shake hands with someone."

Art versus Science

With Haeberle's guidance, I could display a level of confidence that was wiser than my years. Today, I can see that he was teaching us something more than the black-and-white science of business.

Haeberle was paying forward the often unspoken art of entrepreneurship—building relationships, navigating difficult conversations, creating thoughtful presentations. Most business-school programs do not emphasize this. Haeberle was making an investment in the future because he was creating new opportunities. He was allowing for leadership to emerge.

What are you doing to develop and nurture your leadership team?

Looking back, it was this exposure to leadership principles that began to impact what my succession plan would be. Through Haeberle, I learned that the decisions we make about how we lead can create more—or fewer—opportunities in the future. That is, the decisions we make can focus on the *art* of business or the *science* of business; they can be creative, or they can be limiting. I saw that I wanted to create leadership that would instill creative cascades.

The Art of Creative Cascades

By acknowledging the principle that decisions cascade, we see how those decisions we make as leaders have larger ramifications on the journey a business will take. Often we gravitate toward matters directly within the business without developing the trajectory of what will happen *to* the business. That trajectory then churns below the surface, like an avalanche headed for the edge of a cliff. It was in those early days that I began to see each decision as an opportunity to limit or create. And it was from those experiences that I began to observe how to make decisions that would create more opportunity in the future of a business, rather than limiting it.

Here is why this is important: Typically, when business leaders are trying to educate others about how to best create opportunities for the future, we usually focus on the *science* of the business: details, strategy, numbers, client and employee retention. We focus on the way we have done things in the past. Those are the parts that are tactical, factual, and detail oriented. Yet, so much of creating an effective legacy, one that can be harnessed by an incoming leadership team, is learning the *art* of business. What I would challenge you to do instead is to ask yourself, "How am I passing that art along to my leadership team?"

Swimming Pools as Creative Cascades

Rather than sounding too abstract, I want to provide a concrete example.

In the world of swimming-pool design, our goal at Counsilman-Hunsaker was to create memorable, exciting experiences for families, kids, students, and competitors who would be using the venue. However, that experience can't exist in a vacuum, or as one stagnant point in a continuum. An aquatic center is a large investment. It must remain memorable and exciting for generations to come (much like a business). Indeed, we are designing a pool, but we are also creating something that must be sustainable, functional, and relevant for thirty, forty, or fifty years. In those spans of time, things are going to happen in the world that will redefine those spaces in ways we can't predict today. Thus, the actual structure must have enough flexibility to accommodate change.

To embody this principle in the work, we would start our design process with a brainstorm. We tossed around potential ideas to explore new aquatic experiences within a given space, and designed in a way that would accommodate a number of changes that might happen in the future. Once those brainstorms were complete, we would leave extra room in the design: we'd make sure we didn't build out any given space to 100-percent capacity. Those brainstorming sessions about what the space could become in the future became a practical part of the design. Building out the space to 100-percent capacity would undoubtedly limit the ability to expand out the design and adapt.

These design choices were opportunities where decisions could limit what a space could be, or leave room for the unknown. This decision point might not seem critical, but paying attention to how we approach decisions is what leaders must do. These touch points in the day-to-day grind of the business are actually opportunities to limit what future possibilities exist, or expand them. Through my experiences, I have found much to be gained by making the decisions that would create the most options for the future.

It is easy, however, to be romanced by the more limiting option. This is as true in pool projects as it is in business. Often during the design phase of the project, we would be challenged by other professionals who would say, "Let's put in the infrastructure and utilities, because we're already there. We might as well." After completing a few of those projects, we found that rarely do those excess utilities and infrastructures get used. The systems, processes, and technology— even just five years down the road—evolve and become obsolete.

If we had only been focused on the *science* of project completion and full capability, then logic says that building to 100 percent makes sense. But, if we're focused on the *art* of business and if we put on a wider lens, we can leave space for unpredictability.

The principle can be applied to any number of business challenges, particularly how vital it is to create space for new, innovative elements that the future will bring—which clients will want. Instead of heavily investing in finite infrastructure that can't be changed in the future, create space where there are options for the future.

The science of business has the information necessary for a leader to maintain a course of action, keeping the business as is. The art is a fundamental component we must learn and teach to have more options in the future. Create a culture of effective decisionmakers. This affords you the chance to evolve and stay relevant. In any given situation, one is not superior to the other. The point is to not allow yourself to become romanced by "business as usual." It is your role as a legacy-building leader to step back and allow the space for creativity, relationships, and possibility to emerge.

You Will Make Bad Decisions—That Is Not a Bad Thing

The idea of leaving spaces undefined was not brought about just by sheer virtue; it was something we learned at Counsilman-Hunsaker because, in the past, we had made decisions that created limiting cascades.

Learning by making mistakes is part of the experience of making anything worthwhile. That means trying things to see what authentically works and what doesn't. Learning from mistakes acknowledges the idea about learning how to create space for the evolution of a company or project in the future. In the experiences we've had designing pools, we weren't able to learn about the positive ramifications of leaving physical room in the design until we had participated in projects where we built out 100 percent of the space and saw the results. Paying attention to that mistake allowed us to grow our business and evolve past that limiting cascade.

Being conscious of the net effect of your decisions and whether they lean toward limiting or creative cascades does not mean you are never going to fail. However, you will have the knowledge and information to make educated decisions about trying to maximize potential opportunities.

Again, as stated in the previous chapter, "owning" a business really means you own a series of decisions—and each decision matters. It matters because those decisions create cascades. We now understand that each of those cascades can be limiting or creative. Creating a legacy is important to you, so you must be conscious of the kind of cascades you create. Are you leading your team the way that Dr. Haeberle led his young protégés? Are you teaching your would-be leaders the art of the business? If that is what you are doing, then you are creating more options for your uncertain future, i.e., creative cascades. Creative cascades are critical to legacy building because, as we will cover in the next chapter, the future is exceedingly difficult to predict.

CHAPTER 3

YOU CAN'T PREDICT THE FUTURE, BUT YOU CAN HELP CREATE ONE

Despite how many business books espouse the virtues of failure, watching something you care about cease to exist is no fun. When you are in leadership and your business or venture goes sideways in some way you never predicted, you are filled with a deep sense of self-doubt. Failure comes with an emotional (and usually financial) cost to you, your partners, your community, and your family. Truly, it is a special kind of hell. So, why would I or anyone ever say that it is completely worth it?

I can tell you it is not for the romanticized reasons that some thought leaders express. For me, my failures have been worth the effort and investment because they taught me something important about the future. And, more importantly, how my hard-earned understanding about the future became a foundational concept for the shaping of legacy. The most acute example of my failures was a result of what seemed like a wise business move for Counsilman-Hunsaker.

Pivot: A Lesson in Failure

When I began working alongside my father, I remember running into what seemed like an obvious business opportunity. I'd been to numerous meetings where clients expressed a need for gymnasiums, running tracks, and fitness facilities in addition to state-of-the-art pools. At the outset, it looked like there were so many opportunities to expand our scope of services.

We created a plan for a new business called Pivot. The company would define the entire recreation experience, not just pools. When launching a new venture, you have to sell it twice. You have to sell the new concept and explain what it is in a compelling way, then sell why you're the best brand for the job. Keep in mind that we were a group known for our expertise in aquatics, and that new sales challenge proved to be a daunting one.

Roughly three years and several hundred thousand dollars later, it was clear that the venture wasn't working. We pulled the plug.

I still have a few regrets about Pivot's failure, but the experience was unquestionably valuable. We couldn't predict whether it would work or not, but we were exploring opportunities about *how* to grow. The questions we came away with were, How do you grow, invent, and seek new opportunities without putting your entire business at risk? How do you do it in a way that doesn't have the capability to take you out? Those were the kinds of questions we would never have thought to ask had we not tried.

But perhaps the most important thing I learned through this failure was that the future is highly unpredictable. Every planet seemed to be aligned for our success; yet we failed. That moment solidified for me the principle that we cannot predict the future. The emotional and financial debt helped to make that principle stick. That principle would prove critical to our building a leadership bench that could handle uncertainty and change.

Again, I am not telling you something new. But what I hope you begin to do is raise into your consciousness a simple idea: you cannot predict the future. While you may think it to be common knowledge, few business leaders live each day with this seemingly simple idea in mind. Most of us live as though we know what the future will be, but in the light of our experience, we must accept this truth as the next building block to creating a legacy.

How are you teaching your leadership team to explore new opportunities without betting the company on the outcome?

Why You Think Change Is Hard

A lot of business leaders talk to me about how hard it is to change. And, at times, I'm tempted to join in with them. Complaining may be the oldest pastime in business, and complaining about change is almost irresistible. It's just so easy. The swan song of business owners faced with failure tends to include some reference to how much things changed around them or how much they could not get others in the organization to embrace change.

Again, it's tempting. But I don't join in. The truth is that change is not hard—not at all. People resist loss, not change. People, businesses, and industries change all the time, and they do it in spite of challenges.

From my experiences both as an owner and now mentoring owners, I believe the real reason why people believe that change is hard has to do with a misunderstanding about the future. Embracing change and being armed with the proper understanding about the future is crucial to creating a legacy for yourself and for your business.

To best illustrate the misunderstanding of the future, consider this concrete compare-and-contrast leadership model:

1950s "Management by Memo" Model: This leadership style creates a set of best practices for how to run the company, most of which are locked in the mind of the owner. These leaders guard their knowledge like an old recipe book. When they pass it off to the next group of leaders, it goes something like this: *This is perfect. Follow these instructions. Don't mess it up.*

"Legacy Leadership" Model: This leadership style creates a set of best practices for how to run the company, most of which are captured and archived so they can be learned by others. These leaders share their knowledge and ask for insight. When they pass the company off to the next group of leaders, it goes something like this:

This is the best I could do. Adapt it. Change it. I trust you to maximize what is best in it, and the future success is your responsibility.

My experiences have revealed to me that the 1950s management style is the default for many business owners. Perhaps you see some of yourself in that description. These are the leaders that think the future is just the present moment repeated over and over again. "This is the way we have always done it, so this is the way we are always going to do it." With that mindset, any amount of change becomes astonishingly difficult to solve.

The future, in reality, is unpredictable. And that is why a legacy-minded leader seeks to share business knowledge and make innovations. So when—not if—changes occur, your leaders have the ability to successfully manage change. This type of leader embraces the fact that there is uncertainty. It should be obvious by now that a fundamental understanding of what the future is like is critical to creating a lasting, sustainable legacy.

Remember the "creative cascades" from the previous chapter? Those are the decisions we make that give us the most options for the future. If you make decisions that set in motion one limiting cascade after another, you end up with a rigid structure that can be knocked down by any change, be it market trends, staff evolutions, economics, or political climates. When you are in the business of creating a legacy, the more options you have available to you, the better. If you want to shape a successful legacy, or have one at all, you must increase your business's capacity to successfully engage with multiple futures.

Picking Your Future Leader Is a Recipe for Failure

If you are like a lot of business owners I know, you tend to trust your gut on this. You have seen someone on your team who is a top performer, so naturally they will be a great manager of people and strategic thinker, right? Or maybe you are not one of the "trust your instincts" leaders and you use multiple assessment tools, interviews, and evaluations. Surely that level of scrutiny would create increased certainty for determining the new leader.

Maybe you have a markedly different success ratio than we did when I was part of the leadership team at Counsilman-Hunsaker. We found that if a potential leader was anointed based on current leaders' instincts, then that person would have a 20 to 30–percent failure rate in the first year. Sometimes the top performer in our organization was just that. They were a superb engineer or designer, but it turned out they preferred to focus on their craft instead of managing people or leading the organization.

For selecting future business leaders, we found better results at Counsilman-Hunsaker when we created an environment in which would-be leaders self-selected. For us, the best testing ground was our strategic planning process. The goal of the process was to identify who had demonstrated the will and ability to lead. By using strategic planning, we created room for them to succeed or fail on their own merits. And, if they were to fail at certain aspects of the strategic planning process, it would not have dire consequence for the whole business.

Here is what happened: the least obvious leaders began to emerge within the organization. This process proved to be far more effective than the statistical or instinctual models. Part of preparing for the unpredictability of the future means bearing in mind that you can't prescribe how your next team should lead. Yet, I was able to confidently say that I had a team of qualified leaders who could handle an unpredictable future.

How are you identifying those who have the will and ability to lead in your organization?

As with many of the principles that I have outlined, engaging your employees during a strategic planning process is not a unique notion. Scores of thought leaders ask you to do this. The deeper truth I want to reveal to you is that this idea of an unpredictable future is tied to your effectiveness in shaping a legacy. If you hope to create a lasting legacy, then you must find ways to make your present-day systems more flexible and agile. We did not create emerging leadership practices at Counsilman-Hunsaker because we wanted to be trendy; we did it so we could create a legacy for the company, something that could sustain in the face of change.

CHAPTER 4

YOU CAN BE COMFORTABLE BEING UNCOMFORTABLE

After about three hours into the thirty-minute meeting, I looked up from the pile of spreadsheets and notes scattered across my desk. Staring back at me were my two original partners I had identified as the leadership bench at Counsilman-Hunsaker. This was in the fall of 2008. From the time that I had taken ownership of the company in 1999 to 2007, the company had been booming. We had grown by a factor of ten with four new offices and an international presence, and we were poised for more growth—or so I thought.

It was just months before this scene in my office that everyone in the country suddenly became familiar with the term "subprime mortgage." A national housing crisis sent our economy into a recession. The housing market crash sent ripples into the aquatics market, and *our industry contracted by 78 percent.* Imagine: an entire industry operating at 20 percent of its previous capacity. That is enough pressure on leaders to make you reconsider your life choices.

By this point in the conversation, the room was hot. My partners had their sleeves rolled back and stood leaning against their chairs.

How would we survive this? Would people lose their jobs? How many? How can we stay in good condition? We had already let a few people go, and we didn't want to lose more.

Looking back on it, that was the hardest conversation I have ever had in business. And it was, of course, because of the subject matter. There is nothing comfortable when it comes to contracting your business. One option was for me to tell my two partners that my decision about what must be done was final—the buck would stop with me. But that was not the way we agreed to make leadership decisions. What was most important for me in that meeting was that they could understand my reasons for why I wanted to handle our future a certain way. We would not be done with the meeting until there was that level of understanding and agreement.

Tough moments like these are defining for your organization. As leaders, we may intuitively know the best thing for the company at any given time, but I knew that this conversation, as uncomfortable as it was, was necessary. It didn't matter how hot the room got or how draining the dialogue became. There would not be closure until we had an understanding.

In the end, we did cut back—painfully—on staff by 38 percent. As tough as that was, it did not compare to our competitors who either cut back by half or folded their business altogether. More than a year later, when we came out of the recession, our market share grew from 7 percent to 18 percent without taking on debt.

I wanted to tell you about this experience because it is tangible proof of the next foundational principle in creating a legacy: do not allow discomfort to dictate your behavior. I know that is a common saying among businesspeople, but it is especially true in the context of creating your legacy. If what you hope to achieve is something greater and longer lasting than the next fiscal quarter, it is going to mean you will be asked to stretch your comfort zone.

Most business owners I know, when faced with a potentially uncomfortable situation like the one I outlined, will try to exert tighter controls. They will make a series of decisions based upon their gut and exercise authority. I believe there are circumstances in which that leadership style is necessary. However, if you hope to create a legacy for your business, you must lean into the discomfort of engaging your leadership team and others in your decision-making process. This posture creates more options for an uncertain future and better opportunities for a lasting legacy.

Comfort in Numbers

As nice as it would be to think that our performance in the recession was the result of just one uncomfortable conversation, that was not really the case at all. We had been training ourselves on how to deal with discomfort for a long time. That is because years before the word "recession" was ever mentioned, we had started to share our financials with the entire organization.

The decision to share financials is uncomfortable for any leader, but we decided that an open-book approach would be best for namely two reasons.

1. **It builds trust.** When things get rough within the company, sharing the numbers cuts down on the guessing game. If the entire team does not know the status of the company, then they are left to interpret (or misinterpret) subtle body-language cues. That is how rumors get started about layoffs or hidden agendas. With the black-and-white approach, it reduces the emotional drama of business cycles.
2. **It allows for the sharing of decision-making.** So often, companies are in "reaction mode." They are caught off-guard, and the owner is the only one who can make decisions. When you begin to share the numbers, the cycles of business become objective. Then we can begin to work together to maximize profits and minimize losses.

Sharing numbers is not an overnight success. It requires the leadership to create narratives, answer questions, and educate. These are all uncomfortable conversations. Usually this is a process that takes at least six months. I would start with the basics and expand as the understanding of my team increased. When they start asking questions, this is an indication that the seeds you planted months ago are starting to grow. About 60 percent of the companies I mentor today share some form of graphical representation of their budget. Now, I know those uncomfortable conversations make facing something like a recession so much more palatable. If anything, you have a much more objective basis. The decisions for how to minimize the impact of a crisis is shared among a leadership team.

All of this is just best business practice. The magic is how it relates to the creation of a business legacy. The more willing you are to step outside your comfort zone and share knowledge, decision-making, and resources, then the stronger your leadership bench will be. That has value no matter what your definition of a legacy may be.

CHAPTER 5

LEGACY IS NOT ABOUT THE MACHINE—IT'S ABOUT PEOPLE

A very talented and intelligent leader I know, Stephen, heads a construction company. Over his tenure, his business has been successful by virtually every standard. In the short term, his prospects for continued growth are strong, built on handshakes and promises. Stephen is one of those look-you-in-the-eye, trusted people of incredible integrity. The systems he has constructed for client acquisition, sales, and operations are finely tuned. From a purely business-mechanics perspective, he has done and continues to do everything right to build a machine. It functions perfectly as long as he is there to pull the levers. Change occurs when the certainty of pain outweighs the pain of uncertainty.

However, the sad part of this tale is that this owner will not have a legacy. Once he is no longer there to make the machine work, his business will cease to exist. That is because for decades, Stephen has allowed discomfort to dictate his behavior. He kept the highest levels of business knowledge to himself. Fueled by his past success and with the weight of experience, he told others in the company—including his kids—that things must be implemented his way, or they can leave. As a result, there were no prospects of future leadership for anyone in the company.

The dynamic in family business is a tough one. Sometimes the children of the founder want nothing to do with the company because they saw the lifestyle their parents had, and they want nothing to do with that. Sometimes it is the founder who says that his kids deserve something better than the company. The truth is that the option of business ownership is a tremendous gift. That is, as long as what is passed along is not just the machine. If the second generation is given the opportunity to make the business their own, then they can be successful. This opportunity was one of my father's greatest gifts to me.

That is an end that, unfortunately, Stephen did not have the chance to experience. The company was built entirely around the machine and lacks an understanding of the humans who make it thrive. The employees have had no real peer-level relationship with their leader and no sense of depth in their job roles.

The cost of a mindset like this is bigger than it sounds. Stephen, now in his eighties, is at the end of his leadership cycle. He recently had a medical condition that would normally require at least one month of leave, but he was back within three days because the business literally cannot survive without him. That means, as a result of his leadership style, his health is at risk.

I know what you may be thinking: Even if he does not have a leadership bench, he could sell the company to a third party. Sadly, this is not the case either. If he were to attempt to sell the company today, no one would buy it because it relies so heavily on one aging man to make it work. The business offers nothing of deeper significance to its employees. Likewise, there is no upside for savvy outside buyers. There is no legacy.

My hope is that Stephen can prompt you to ask yourself some hard questions about the kind of leadership you are providing. I share this story with you to make clear that we are talking about principles that are deeper at a more earnest level. So far, the principles set down are nothing new. Being long-term and strategic in decision-making, accepting uncertainty, leaning into discomfort—all of these topics are covered in the world of business thought leadership. However, if Stephen's example means anything, it means that these principles are not superficial. They are not trendy business topics created to sell books. Following and understanding them creates the capacity for something bigger than you. And, if that is what you hope to achieve, then the key to that legacy is not in the machine you build. It is in your people.

The Legacy of the Machine

This business model for my contractor friend contains a grave, powerful lesson: the legacy of a machine is merely what it does. Machines do not change. They cannot adapt to new circumstances or face an uncertain future. People do that.

Stephen is a poster child for the 1950s "Management by Memo" leader outlined previously. His secretary still takes notes for him in shorthand and uses green ledger paper for accounting. There's still a Rolodex of contacts on his desk. He used to be a stalwart rotary-phone user, but they have finally upgraded to the modern invention of a push-button landline. His business is utterly stuck in the time during which it was founded, and the owner has been completely unwilling to share anything about what has made the company successful. He is trying—in vain—to protect those he cares about from the stress of ownership. Yet in reality, he is placing them at risk.

Family members growing up in the business didn't see a place for themselves in its leadership. How could they, when he kept the knowledge to himself? Many grew apart from the business and became successful on their own. The company does have an illustrious history and a structure well worth passing on to the next generation, but the owner has rebuffed his children's attempts to help him. He is afraid to change the recipe book. No effort has been made to create a succession plan, and no leaders have risen to the top to take it over and carry on the company legacy.

The resultant business is a structure that has remained ignorant of the axioms we have covered thus far. The ironic thing is, from outward appearances, all is well. The machine is running. Tragically, many business leaders think this way. Perhaps you have been victim of this thinking, as well. The choice to work on building a legacy is much farther-reaching than a vain attempt to preserve your contribution.

Creating Ownership Mindset Gives You Options

As business owners, we owe it to ourselves and to the families of the people who have joined with us in our endeavors to make a sincere effort to set up our companies to achieve the highest level of success. We do this not because it is easy or comfortable, but because that is what the others who have joined us in our journey deserve.

The best way that I have found to do this is through the creation of ownership thinking and opportunity for every person who emerges as a leader. If the aforementioned owner had instead made the choice to invest in his team, where would his business prospects be today? What if he had created a leadership team that could carry on the organization without his daily presence? The fate of his company and legacy would likely be much different.

Accepting this truth as a business leader in your day-to-day practice does not mean you have to nail down every piece of what the business apparatus should look like. It means your goal is to nurture your employees and the people around you so that they can build out a skill set that allows them to make good decisions. Allowing people to innovate upon your original design makes the company more agile. In the case of the construction contractor—if his business is to survive in the future, it will not be through a process that honors his legacy. It will be because someone revamped it and took it in an entirely new direction.

This isn't to say that the machine of your business does not matter. However, as we've witnessed over and over, those machines cannot create a legacy solely on their own, because they cannot change on their own. Humans are what bring innovation to machines, not the other way around. Humans are the only component of that equation with the capability to respond creatively when the landscape changes.

Creating Leaders Creates Value, Which Creates Legacy

By creating a leadership team with an ownership mindset, you can step outside of the company and it will continue to run without needing your skills and leadership for it to survive.

It is no small coincidence that this also increases the value of your organization in the eyes of a third party. Someone else who has interest in possibly purchasing your business is going to immediately understand that the business is worth more if it has been built with longevity in mind. Value increases if they know they don't need the owner peering over their shoulder for five years. If you understand that people are more important than the machine, then that transfer of institutional knowledge and business savvy will have already occurred.

As a leader, you have the option to structure your company so that it is about the people who run it, rather than the machine they run. The people around you will be able to feel the difference. They will learn to trust you more deeply, which further opens up your options as a leader. As this process unfolds, your leadership team will self-identify and tell you who they are.

Leadership is about managing change—anticipating it, reacting to it, moving through it, adapting to it. Navigating all of those elements of change successfully requires you to have built out a team of people you trust. The potential to do something great with your business machine will always depend on how it relates to the people who run it. When those tools work together in tandem with your leadership team, you are empowering your legacy to continue long after you are no longer around to protect its fate.

Intermission

Plans are nothing; planning is everything.
—Dwight D. Eisenhower

Taken at face value, many of the principles you have seen in this book are likely not novel to you. They are the conversation topics of endless conferences, books, and articles. A lot of business owners know what would be "good" for them. Few, however, actually attempt a plan.

In my experience, the issue is not a lack of knowledge, drive, or savvy. The thing that is missing is a compelling reason to take your business thinking and behavior to the next level. If you knew that each behavior you chose to act out was tied to a desired outcome, then you would be more likely to implement that outcome. For me, the most compelling reason was the creation of a legacy. After I left my leadership role, I wanted something to live on that would bring meaning to others and continue the tradition set in motion so many years ago by my father. Unless I changed everything about how we were conducting business at Counsilman-Hunsaker, then I knew there was no chance I would have a legacy.

The idea I hope you are starting to understand is everything you do creates a legacy. Experience has revealed to me that every move you make affects what you will leave behind. While you can't plan the exact shape of your legacy, the act of planning in an effective way will create the foundation for your legacy.

If the notions outlined so far have made you feel uneasy, here's an even deeper truth for you: No one will want to own or purchase your business unless you take action now. Think about it. An internal ownership candidate will not risk their financial future, time, and treasure if they think they lack the business knowledge and savvy to be successful. And that is why, if a legacy matters to you at all, you must take action.

What I Did

The good news is that there are five steps to transfer the institutional knowledge and business savvy to the next leadership team. These steps are all about giving ownership candidates the information they need to be able to become entrepreneurs. They are designed so you can teach emerging leaders how to take risks and "put it on the line."

1. **Have authentic conversations.** These are more than just cultural window dressings. Everyone in the company must be on the same side of the table when facing challenges or addressing the future of the company.
2. **Identify your leadership team bench.** Within your company right now, there is leadership latent within key employees. You must create an environment where they demonstrate a will and ability to lead.
3. **Transfer knowledge.** The worst place to store business knowledge is in your head. You must create structures that allow for knowledge transfer.
4. **Encourage innovation, not guardianship.** A successful business will remain successful until something changes— and things always change. You must build in leadership that can manage change.
5. **Trust with confidence.** Trusting with confidence happens when people start acting like (and becoming) real owners.

Using these tools, you'll end up with employees who are able to bring about solid results in the face of uncertainty. Rather than planning a steadfast structure, empowering future leaders with tools, knowledge, and support means a better chance of maneuvering through uncertain times. Your job is to create the kinds of leaders who encourage the best performance possible for their team, increasing the overall value for you and your company.

No amount of planning will give you the perfect plan. The following are things we implemented at Counsilman-Hunsaker and some of the tools my colleagues have tried. My hope is that these are helpful tools which can move your business forward and connect you to a new way of thinking about how to lead your organization.

PART II

CHAPTER 6

HAVE AUTHENTIC CONVERSATIONS

KEY TAKEAWAYS

- ✓ Create a "we" instead of an "us vs. them" mentality.
- ✓ Show the numbers.
- ✓ Transfer your instincts.

In the business world, people talk a lot about honesty. Many companies, big or small, cite integrity or transparency as a core value. You might even see an inspirational poster about it hanging on the wall of their conference room, and when they bring on new employees they will talk about how much they value real communication. But from what I have witnessed, talk is where honesty ends. Very rarely does honesty or authenticity make its way into practice. We say honesty but don't do honesty. Even at the leadership level, we hold back on knowledge or don't engage in a way that is real.

I do not believe this happens because people want to lie. I believe it is because most leaders do not know how or where their aspiration of authenticity would take place. If you hope to create the kind of legacy that lives on after you, then the first step is to have authentic conversations. But just what does that mean in the context of your business? How do we *do* honesty?

A Late-Night Phone Call from a Friend

A friend of mine, Robert, knows exactly what doing honesty and having authentic conversations mean. Back in the '70s, he founded a construction company on the West Coast. At the time, he had a wife and growing family. The demands of making a business thrive meant he was under constant pressure to devote his energy into his work. He grew the way most founders do: through sheer grit and determination of will. He worked nights, weekends, holidays. And, within just a few years, he was becoming an influential company in his industry.

Thirty years later, after a divorce and the fatigue of growing a company to more than $80 million in annual revenues, Robert called me. He was in pain—a kind that few can know. It is the pain of not knowing what the legacy of the business was to be. It is a mixture of mortality, doom, and dread. The person whom he had foreseen as the heir apparent for the business, his son, was injured badly in an accident. Watching his son suffer from life-altering injuries was bad enough, but Robert's pain was compounded by the fact that his daughter, Dawn, had no experience in the contracting industry. The whole future and livelihood of his family was suddenly being called into question.

Worse yet, he realized that his company could not function without him. This realization threatened his view of the company, leadership, and himself as a person. The company *was* him. If the company could not function without him, nothing could continue after he exited. All of the work he had done to design and build something would be scrapped. The hours, the money, the struggles, and the fighting would all be in vain. It also meant that the employees and their families were counting on him to know what to do next.

As I said, Robert was in a special kind of pain.

Even if you are not facing the crossroads that Robert has faced, being a business owner means some clammy, sweaty nights pouring over numbers, projections, and employee challenges. You know what it is like to know so many people are counting on you. The pain that Robert was feeling, however, is a legacy pain. It is especially acute because it feels beyond your control and far too difficult to overcome. However, it *can* be overcome if you are willing to take the first step: having authentic conversations.

Robert called me on that day because we are old friends, and he had seen the work that we were doing at Counsilman-Hunsaker around building up a leadership team. We talked about what he really wanted and his vision for the future. He didn't want to sell to a third party, because he felt that threatened the core of the company, and, ideally, he wanted to create something that could support generations of his family to come. But just what was the path to making that happen? How would he teach Dawn fast enough, and would the management team trust her?

I started working with Robert in the same place where I started creating a legacy at Counsilman-Hunsaker. We started creating authentic conversations.

Getting on One Side of the Table

Ten years before I sold to the leadership team at Counsilman-Hunsaker, I had pains that were similar to Robert's. They were not nearly as pronounced, but they were related to the future of the company. I found that strategic planning was especially difficult when I was the one who had the knowledge about the finances of the business, the industry trends, and how managing for growth functions. This placed me on one side of the table all by myself and in an adversarial position to everyone else. I had to find a way to bring everyone on one side of the table. The best way I found to do that was to have authentic conversations about every aspect of the business, including finances.

Authentic conversations mean a complete shift in the conversation with the people touched by your business, employees and partners alike. It means talking about the financial future of the company and what that means to everyone involved. It means sharing business information with everyone and teaching the art of the decision-making process, not just the answer. Authentic conversations allow for the emergence of the most talented, insightful people to join in the leadership.

Authentic conversations break through one of the most common issues in business: "us" versus "them." That is, management versus team, owner versus employees. It even happens between divisions. Authentic conversations, because they are based on information and not opinions, get everyone on one side of the table. They are the way we can all look at business challenges together.

And there is no topic that shifts a conversation to one side of the table faster than money.

Share the Numbers

Conversations about money are one of the most mishandled concepts by even seasoned business executives and leaders. The reason for this misunderstanding is not a lack of intelligence or patience; it is because no one has taught the leadership team how to interpret the data. No one gave them something meaningful that met them where they were.

One of the most powerful tools we implemented at Counsilman-Hunsaker was a company dashboard. Everyone on the team could access it. It aggregated financial information into a graph that showed employees whether business was trending up or down. It was a very simple, powerful way to keep everyone informed, and, most importantly, it allowed everyone to look forward. The purpose for sharing information is to allow everyone to make knowledgeable decisions. You likely have a good gut instinct on where the business is headed. The most valuable thing that you can pass along to your next leadership team is a glimpse of that instinct.

CORPORATE DASHBOARD

REVENUE / EXPENSES

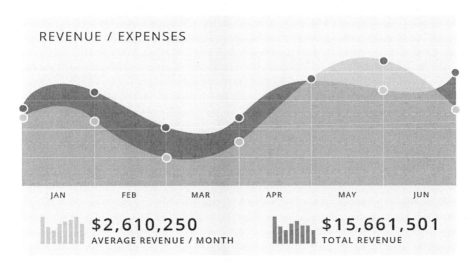

JAN   FEB   MAR   APR   MAY   JUN

$2,610,250
AVERAGE REVENUE / MONTH

$15,661,501
TOTAL REVENUE

KEY PERFORMANCE INDICATORS

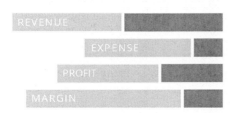

REVENUE
EXPENSE
PROFIT
MARGIN

3,125

NUMBER OF UNITS SOLD

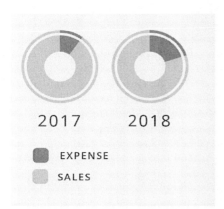

2017   2018

EXPENSE
SALES

PROJECTIONS

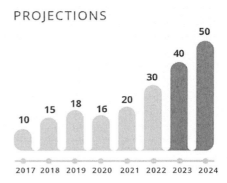

10   15   18   16   20   30   40   50

2017 2018 2019 2020 2021 2022 2023 2024

Sharing financial numbers is counterintuitive for most business owners. By keeping the numbers under lock and key, we lose the ability to teach the next leadership team how to manage through common business cycles. Many new owners suffer from "lineal budgeting." They believe that whatever financial circumstances happened most recently are going to continue to happen. So, if you lost 10 percent of revenue last year, then there is this Eeyore effect. You contract the business, fire people, and cut back on expenses. But anyone seasoned in business knows that there is a cycle. There is expansion and contraction. Almost all of it is completely out of your control. Having the data to make that cycle tangible means that you can look forward as a company, all on one side of the table. Everyone will see the trends. Then you can have the confidence to invest in the company even when things are bad and to make shrewd decisions when things are at their peak.

Your job as the business leader is to create a team that will maximize the business-cycle peaks and minimize the valleys. Instead of chasing a trend or scrambling to get ahead, you can make authentic conversations happen about the future of the company. While you cannot predict the future, you can forecast it with confidence. The forecasts will not be 100 percent correct, but that is not the point. The point is, you will have your group of leaders that are not stuck in today. Your team is now thinking six months to three years ahead. Creating a team with that level of strategic decision-making is necessary for a legacy.

If only partners or C-suite executives have access to top-level information, how can you expect an employee to successfully participate in your leadership team? They'll have no frame of reference to interpret what they'll need to know, and it will be nearly impossible for them to carry your legacy forward. Providing employees with a company dashboard means you have your would-be leaders anticipating and poised for change.

Just how you decide to share your numbers and in what fashion you do is up to you. There are a number of philosophies on exactly how to do it. At Counsilman-Hunsaker, we created our own system for open-book management, one that made the most sense for our leadership and company culture. We combined the best thinking from Kraig Kammer's *CEO Tools*, Jack Stack's *Great Game of Business*, and our own combined business backgrounds.

As with most of the practices that helped us to create a legacy at Counsilman-Hunsaker, there was nothing revolutionary in our practices. What became clear is that implementing a practice like open-book management into our firm was more than just great business leadership, employee retention, and engagement. It created the platform on which we could have authentic conversations. It was the meat of those kinds of conversations that shaped our team's mindset and allowed for leaders to emerge.

Developing Leadership Instincts

In addition to understanding financial numbers, there is something else that likely separates you from your employees: instinct. You have a sixth sense about the health of the company and where it can grow. That instinct was critical to carrying your company to where it is today. But if you hope to leave a legacy or have success beyond your present day, you have to somehow develop the leadership instincts of your team. They have to have a gut for business, too.

Much like Dr. Haeberle did for me so many years ago, I began to find ways that I could transfer the art and not just the science of business. We needed a team that could be agile and think about the future of the business on a level that was bigger than their particular role in the business.

At Counsilman-Hunsaker, the path to authentic conversations about this kind of instinct was using narratives. The two things that predicted our future were new home sales and educational spending. When we would create visualizations of new-home starts on top of our revenue numbers, the correlation was striking. What this visualization did was give emerging leadership a real, information-based way to develop their own gut for business. It also meant that we could better prepare for likely futures—even the ugly ones—in a more efficient way. No longer was I the lone person watching out over the horizon. When the housing market crashed in 2008, we had a whole team that could ready us to weather the storm.

If you want your legacy to continue, you must create a narrative and educate others about what affects your business. The narrative must be based on real information. It will help your leadership team to develop the kinds of instincts they need in order to manage change.

You may already have in mind the trends that most deeply affect your revenues. If none are coming to mind at the moment, there are a number of ways you can figure out what related industries or market behaviors you can use as a source for your narrative. Often there are industry-related trade associations or publications that hold forecasting summits, and you can turn to a trusted peer network for deeper sources. In addition, and in light of the understanding you have about your business, take time to reflect on your experiences as you have grown. What were the most ideal conditions that were present in the market for your expansion? What was a common reason for your business to be challenged that was out of your control? The point is that you want to transfer what you already can sense to your leadership team. Armed with that narrative, they can begin to understand the art of business in addition to its science and make more informed decisions about the future.

From "I Think" to "I Know"

You're likely starting to see a trend in this chapter, and you probably see what I mean when I say authentic conversations. The idea is to take what is usually nebulous or difficult to articulate and present it in a way that is as concrete as possible. This allows for a conversation on a different basis, one that is larger than egos or emotional whims. It is about everyone looking at the same set of data or visualizations and allowing that to shape the conversation.

One area that tends to remain abstract for most businesses has to do with customer and employee satisfaction. Most business owners would like to believe they have happy customers and engaged employees. Perhaps that is true for you, but most have no real basis for this feeling. That's because they never bothered to ask. Some of the fear about facing this is that it can reveal some truths you did not expect, and asking people for an honest appraisal opens up issues you may want to avoid.

We implemented both employee and customer surveys at Counsilman-Hunsaker. What that enabled us to do was create conversations based on data. We could pull a project lead aside and ask questions based on the feedback we received. If it appeared a customer was not happy, we could ask them what they thought about that. Their answers revealed their level of engagement and readiness for leadership. They may get defensive, or they may have a compelling reason. Either way, the conversation was based on data and not on feelings. It was authentic.

EMPLOYEE SURVEYS

Conduct these annually, share them with your team, and track multiple years of data.

SURVEY TOPICS

✓ Leadership
✓ Mission and values
✓ Governance and accountability
✓ High-performance work
✓ Working environment

✓ Trust
✓ Employee engagement
✓ Satisfaction
✓ Development
✓ Legal and ethics

IDENTIFY OPPORTUNITY FOR IMPROVEMENT

IMPLEMENT

CREATE SITUATION REPORT

FLYWHEEL OF CHANGE

DECISION

DECISIONMAKING PROCESS

RESEARCH

More clearly than any other exercise, these surveys allowed us to make a leap from "I think" to "I know" as it related to our company's growth. We turned decision-making into something that was based on data instead of momentary impulse. It made for increased cohesion in the team, and it meant that we held each other accountable to backing up our decisions with the most tangible information. Instead of mere speculation, we were leaders armed with the most knowledge we could get to make informed decisions—about the future of the company, the customer experience, and our respective roles in it.

Personally, surveys also revealed trends in my own leadership. I saw that there were areas, especially early on in the process, where I was more challenged. The first several times we implemented employee surveys, I felt deeply uncomfortable. It was not easy to absorb feedback. But leaning into this discomfort proved to be a game-changer for everyone involved in helping us create a legacy at Counsilman-Hunsaker.

Creating Transparency Is Critical to Legacy

Creating transparency through conversation, new dynamics, and sharing information is the touchstone that helped us create a company culture that is still a source of pride for me. If you hope to leave a legacy, you must shift from being the kind of owner who *talks* about authenticity to one who *has* authenticity. You must get real. You do this by creating the systems that allow people to look forward together. Those systems need to be based on the real issues and data that affect the customers and the team. It is not good enough to just act on instinct; you must create a new basis for how to talk about the future of the company if you hope to create a leadership bench and have a legacy.

Another Phone Call from a Friend

Five years after that initial late-night phone call from Robert, he called me again. But this time, the tone was very different. "Scot, I'm leaving my lawyer's office. We just completed the transfer of ownership to Dawn and my employees," he said. "Thank you. I could not have done it without you."

While this was reaffirming to hear, I did want to qualify Robert's placement of gratitude. "That is awesome news, Robert. I am so happy for you, Dawn, your family, and your business. But the thanks really go to you and your leadership team. This was not an easy road, but you stuck to what mattered most to you."

In the preceding five years, Robert had implemented all of the processes necessary to have authentic conversations with his team. They opened the books for the first time. They created narratives about the future, and they began to survey their customers and employees. They did the hard work you read about in this chapter.

As they proceeded through strategic planning and some steps you will see in the following chapters, a leadership team began to emerge that included Dawn, his daughter. In short time they had the resources necessary to take the leadership helm. This meant that Robert's vision for his business could live on. It meant that the employees and their families had a sustainable and meaningful livelihood. Similar to the acuteness of the legacy pain I described, the feeling of accomplishment at creating a legacy is immeasurable. It is one that you can experience as well if you are willing to take the first step: have authentic conversations.

ACTION PLAN

- ✓ Investigate open-book management techniques. You can start with Jack Stack's *The Great Game of Business.* Find a model that works for you.
- ✓ Create data-based narratives about your business to transfer your instincts. Look for industries that have the most influence on your revenues.
- ✓ Find a way to begin taking stock of your employee and customer satisfaction. This can be simple. The point is that you make a beginning.

CHAPTER 7

IDENTIFY YOUR LEADERSHIP TEAM BENCH

KEY TAKEAWAYS

- ✓ Create a structure where those would-be leaders can emerge.
- ✓ Allow for self-selection of the team.
- ✓ Lead change on a strategic level, not a tactical level.

During my time as a business owner, I saw many of my colleagues fall victim to a common trap: attempting to predict future leaders. We have previously discussed the futility of trying to predict the future, but often our inclination to try to control the future can be so strong. So, this lesson is worth repeating. A fair number of business leaders often believe they are endowed with some special intuition about selecting future leaders. They trust their instincts to predict the next influential leaders of the organization. However, the reality is that even the best of us are correct just over 50 percent of the time— not great odds when you're betting the company's future.

What is your hit rate for hiring the right person?

Incorrectly designating company leaders causes chaos and pain for the organization, and that's just in the short term. If you hope to create a lasting legacy within your industry, it is far better to focus your attention on something over which you actually have influence: creating a culture in which leaders can emerge.

Leadership Where You Least Expected It

Back in 2000, Counsilman-Hunsaker was in need of a receptionist. After our interview process, we found Macy was the best fit for the position. It would be an understatement to say that she was inexperienced in the industry. From day one, however, she displayed a natural curiosity for how the business worked and, most importantly, how it could be improved and what role she could play in that improvement.

Very quickly, Macy's role within the company began to change. In a couple of years, she was helping us manage events and customer experiences. She had a talent for spotting ways that the customer experiences could be improved, and then working to implement ways to make those improvements happen. She did this with little need for instruction or oversight despite her lack of experience.

As we began to have authentic conversations at Counsilman-Hunsaker, we saw the need to formalize the process of finding emerging leaders in the organization. There were people who excelled at thinking about the future of the company, so we needed a place for them to have influence—not because of their title or tenure, but because they demonstrated the will and ability to lead. My partners and I decided that the strategic planning process was the best experiential way that emerging leaders could shape the future of the organization.

In one of the first conversations about our new strategic planning process I had with my partners, we identified that Macy was one of those kinds of people. She had a sense for finding ways to continuously improve processes. We felt she was ready for a seat at the table.

Just three years after she was hired to be our receptionist, Macy was part of our strategic planning team. Through her research and dedication to helping us grow, she helped to formalize our strategic improvement and management processes. Perhaps less obvious on paper, but unavoidable in experience, Macy had a tendency to be optimistic—to expect the best of herself and others. She was inspiring. This kind of artful leadership ability was not a theory; we could see it displayed. She leaned into leadership situations that likely caused her discomfort, but she did them with a kind of passion that made every interaction with her meaningful and engaging.

Little did we know at the time that this was just the beginning of Macy's leadership role at Counsilman-Hunsaker.

Allow for Leaders to Emerge

It is not lost on me that we were lucky to have a person like Macy in our company. A-players like that are hard to find—and that is just the point. How often do we overlook people who have the leadership ingredients but nowhere to go with them? This does not happen because we do not care, but because there is no basis or path to leadership outside of pure instinct.

This matters in the context of building a legacy for your organization. No matter what you may decide you would like to do with your business, there is a need for knowledgeable leaders who know how to make decisions.

To find the leaders like Macy within Counsilman-Hunsaker, we built upon the structures we already had in place when we had authentic conversations. We used a combination of the corporate dashboard, SWOT (strengths, weaknesses, opportunities, threats) analysis, employee surveys, and customer surveys and created a strategic planning group. By using the activities associated with strategic planning, we found a way to engage people in ways that were challenging, but did not set them up for failure.

Through trial and error, we found that strategic planning is best done with no more than ten people total to promote some intimacy and not a public speaking forum. I also made sure, as the CEO, that I listened more than I talked. This was not easy for me. We wanted to create our collective plan and not mine. I wanted to observe how they dealt with adversity, being challenged, and how they thought through their portion of the plan.

As a concept, strategic planning has been around since before the Great Depression. Using the concepts involved in plotting the growth of a business is a hundred-year-old idea. At this point, there are as many ways to strategically plan as there are privately held companies. It is nothing new. The nuance I want you to grab ahold of is using strategic planning as a tool for creating a legacy. It is the *why* behind the strategic planning. This is the best tool that we found for allowing the cream to rise to the top—for leaders to emerge. At Counsilman-Hunsaker, we decided that strategic planning was the most fitting leadership training ground for legacy creation. We did not want to make people *feel like* leaders; we wanted them to have a chance to really *be* leaders. We wanted them to put their ideas to the test. Being able to strategically plan for the future is a prerequisite for ownership. So, why not use that critical skill as a way to identify the next crop of leaders?

Create Accountability: Walk the Walk, and Talk the Talk

With an eye toward the legacy that we were attempting to create, we set out to foster an environment where leaders could emerge. Accountability and trust were critical, so we created rules of engagement for the strategic planning process.

One example was our three-strike rule. We had no problem with modifying the strategic plan if team members found better information. However, anyone who wanted to make a modification to the strategic plan would need to bring it to the group two weeks before it was due. If a team member brought in changes the morning it was due or missed it, we'd call that a "strike." That meant there was a tangible moment we could point to in which the team member did not meet expectations, reinforcing the principle of holding each other accountable. This meant the team, not the CEO, held each other accountable for changes, progress, and thinking strategically.

One strike meant the team member had to buy donuts for the strategic planning team—not a big deal, but it helped manifest accountability all the same. For the second strike, the team member had to buy lunch for the whole company. We had several offices established by that point, so the team member would be shipping pizza all over the United States. They would also have to disclose why the commitment didn't happen to the entire company—a humbling prospect. The third time a team member got a strike, they weren't invited back to be a part of the strategic planning team.

It may seem harsh, but what really happens is that the cream rises to the top. The people with real leadership abilities emerge, and the nonleaders self-select out.

Opting Out of Leadership

Since we had a rules-based strategic planning environment based on accountability, we quickly identified people who did not have the will and ability to lead. Their exit from the strategic planning team could take place in a way that was objective and fair. We found that people who opted out of leadership fell, generally, into one of three categories:

1. **Not Willing**

   One employee came to me after being on the strategic planning team for six or seven months. He was an engineer and corporate-knowledge library and had earned his seat as part of the leadership team. However, he told me that he was just not at all comfortable with the responsibility. He loved being an engineer and wanted to be an engineer. He asked me if he could just go back to doing that. Of course I obliged, and we were able to set him on a course for his career in an honorable way.

   This kind of thing happened on more than one occasion. It gave us confidence that we were putting people to the right kind of test. On paper, our engineer was perfect for leadership. But if he was not ready to be comfortable being uncomfortable, then his ability to lead with confidence would be compromised. How often does this happen within the context of a legacy? The owner leaves the responsibility to people who, quantitatively, seem up to the task, but, in actuality, they are not willing to do what it takes to be in leadership.

At first the people who opted out of the plan gave me a sense of discouragement. I wanted them to be a part of it. But eventually I found that letting people opt out is a great thing. While they had the capabilities, they did not have the willingness to be leaders. We were able to place our library of knowledge in a position where he could have the highest and best use without reservation.

2. **Not Able**

Then there were the harder cases of people who thought they had what it took, but they just didn't. They were honest and hardworking, but they could not perform strategically enough to meet their goals on a consistent basis. These people are more difficult because their aspirations are higher than their capabilities. As the owner, this group is harder than the first to lead. You must, however, make the decision for their reassignment, one that is team-based and balanced. What you risk by allowing them to stay on is much greater than what you risk if they decide to leave your company.

3. **The Talker**

The toughest case, however, is the employee I call "The Talker." This is the person who, to put it kindly, is adept at self-promotion. Yet for all of their talk, they can rarely follow through with anything that looks like leadership. They miss deadlines, and they discourage or hold back other people on the team. They are all talk and no action. You cannot depend on them. These people are the toughest because they are suffering from the idea that they are both willing and able. And they are neither. The strategic planning team was usually quick to find these people, because the process revealed their character and capabilities quickly.

While all of these cases were not comfortable to deal with, they were best dealt with as a part of the strategic planning context. It exposed when a person was not the type for leadership. No matter what their job performance may have suggested, they did not have what it takes to deal with strategic challenges and managing change.

When it comes down to it, that is what you need in a leader— someone who can anticipate and manage change. If they cannot make it through a strategic planning group process, they are not up for the task. Therefore, you're creating a more agile company if you allow for nonleaders to self-select out. What you are also doing is using strategic planning as a process for finding the characteristics you will most need in a leadership team. No matter what the transactional outcome is—sale to employee or family or a third party—that is the team that will be leading the changes to come.

Solving the Problems You Should Be Solving

You do not need to create the strategic planning team process or rules as we did. That is not the point. The real question for you as the leader in your organization is, How are you identifying the people who have the will and ability to lead? Again, the planning is more important than the plan. While you do not have to follow this formula, you must create an environment where leaders can emerge if you hope to create a legacy.

If you can successfully create this kind of environment, it also means that you begin to solve the kinds of problems that you should be solving. It means that you are focused on the creation of that environment and playing the role of advisor. At this point in the development of your legacy, you will have had authentic conversations about the financial future of the company and about how to develop a leadership instinct. You will have also created an environment where leaders can emerge and nonleaders can self-select out. They now know what behaviors it takes to lead an organization.

An Unlikely, Effective Leader Emerges

Those leadership behaviors—both the tangible and the intangible— were the kinds of characteristics the strategic planning team saw in Macy. In the years she spent on the strategic planning team, our company grew because of the kinds of processes she was able to champion. The strategic planning team decided to match Macy's ambition, and the company paid for her to get her undergraduate degree. Soon after, she became the director of the design studio and responsible for managing a healthy portion of the people and resources in the business.

In typical Macy fashion, she excelled at her leadership role. A recent former employee remarked of Macy, "Macy was one of the best bosses that I've ever had . . . always smiling, and really made me feel like a part of the team. Very conscientious and always looking to improve."

Eight years after we hired her as our receptionist, I sat across the table from Macy. In front of me were the documents needed to bring Macy onto the ownership team. In just under a decade, she went from entry level to owner. Imagine what you are communicating if you were to have a path to leadership like that in your company.

ACTION PLAN

✓ Identify the qualities you believe a leader should have. You can begin with the ones you have seen in the first half of this book, but they should be yours.

✓ Research the strategic planning process. You can also call on several consultants who can customize the experience for you.

✓ Find ways to make the path to emerging leadership transparent in the organization.

CHAPTER 8

TRANSFER KNOWLEDGE

KEY TAKEAWAYS

- ✓ The worst place to store knowledge is in your own head.
- ✓ Knowledge is not power. Sharing knowledge is power.
- ✓ You must share both the science and the art of business to create a foundation for legacy.

I know there are so many things that have kept you up at night. I am not talking about barking dogs or noisy neighbors. I mean the real sleep-killers: a drop in monthly sales, an emerging threat to your industry, and mistakes you have made. To be a business owner is to suffer periodic insomnia. That is something they do not tell you in business school.

Some nights you rise and work into the early morning hours. An inspiration will surely arise if you just work harder and apply yourself more, you suppose. Multiple pots of coffee later, you emerge, sometimes with a new resolution, sometimes with inspiration, and sometimes with nothing but fatigue. And now you must face your day.

But in your toiling, you have learned something. If nothing else, you gained some insights of what does not satisfy as a solution. The knowledge you possess has something to do with both the science and art of business. And now that knowledge—that hard-fought wisdom you gained from years of tireless effort—is locked inside your head. Unfortunately, that is where the knowledge remains in most companies.

That outcome would be acceptable if the only person responsible for growing the company is you. But if you hope to create a legacy and a team of capable leaders, then your head is the worst place to store knowledge. It must be transferred to the team in a useful and meaningful way. Now you have a leadership team that has been tested through strategic planning. They have the will and ability to lead. Your challenge at this stage of legacy creation is to share your knowledge with that team so they have a foundation for decision-making that is deep, effective, and proven.

Creating Consistency in Success

A few years ago, I was introduced to someone who faced this challenge of transferring knowledge, and she did so bravely. Tara is a founding owner of a residential-restoration company. She founded her franchise in the Midwest more than twenty years ago and has expanded to ten locations with over five hundred employees. Most of her success has been due to the trust she has built within the networks of other complementary businesses—real estate companies, contractors, builders, and other emergency services.

When I met her, she was getting ready to retire. With a mountain of knowledge and experience and a track record of success, she had initially thought the next stage of business—transferring the business to a third party—would be achievable within a couple of years. But the valuation and audit of her company revealed a lack of consistency among her locations. She also discovered a lack of understanding what management of people and resources means among the leadership team.

While I knew Tara hoped to retire within months, I implored her to take a step back. Even if Tara had hoped to sell to a third party, she needed a leadership team that could perform consistently and with some degree of process uniformity. A team like that would increase the confidence of a potential buyer. Most of the growth mindset and knowledge were still inside Tara's head. Transferring that to an emerging leadership team would create a much more attractive opportunity for a buyer.

Tara and I started with authentic conversations. We created a dashboard and a way to visualize her instincts about business into narratives. What quickly became evident is that while she was expert in her industry, Tara had never really empowered her leaders to think with an ownership mindset. They had never had to digest numbers, forecast numbers, or take quantitative feedback. It was at that point that Tara realized that we were in for more of a journey than she had realized. The path to her legacy felt tenuous, but we pressed on.

From there, we moved on to identifying her leadership bench. Even though Tara had already handpicked leaders based on tenure, we implemented a strategic planning process to allow for those who had the will and ability to lead to emerge. What happened next surprised Tara. Over one-third of her handpicked leaders opted out of the strategic planning role. For me, this reinforced the fact that you cannot choose the leaders, and the path was cleared for motivated leaders to emerge.

I should reiterate: Tara is a successful business owner by nearly any measure. She has been relentless in growing her business, earning millions in annual revenues. But just like so many of us, she did this largely in a vacuum. While she followed conventional wisdom and best practices, she still was left with much to accomplish when she was closing in on retirement. This is important because while the practices I suggest are not revolutionary, they are not instinctual for most leaders. Moreover, they are not conventional business wisdom. What I worked to impress upon Tara and what I hope you are seeing is that your legacy is being created right now. If you hope to have any influence on creating the one you want, you must completely change your approach to leadership and to where knowledge about being an effective leader is stored.

Shortly after the fallout from the strategic plan, we started creating for Tara something called a "master toolbox." It is a technique that proved to be effective in transferring knowledge for the leadership team at Counsilman-Hunsaker.

The Master Toolbox, the Science of Business

Every business has certain processes and pieces of wisdom that need to be captured and codified in ways that are easy to find and understand to be meaningful. At one point in Counsilman-Hunsaker's history, it seemed like we had three companies in one. Depending upon the person you asked, you had very different specifications, and the appearance of the drawings and details were not unified. This made for a lack of efficiencies, not to mention some issues with customer and employee experience.

The goal was to capture the best thinking in the organization as it related to repeated processes. For us, a large portion of this toolbox, which was accessible digitally by anyone in the organization, was made up of detailed processes for different types of pools. We outlined the exact deliverable with drawings and details, and came up with a master process. That way, the next team tasked with a similar project had a thorough record of deliverables from those who had come before them. We included how the team achieved goals, how they came to decisions, and why they made those decisions. This was a helpful exercise in generating relationships between team members and making sure everyone is on the same page.

We made the process of creating an entry for the master toolbox part of the close of each project. That way, if there was something that needed to be added, it was captured while it was still fresh in the minds of the team. This information could then be reviewed by our management team and modified if necessary.

I wish I could tell you that the process ran smoothly and it suddenly increased our productivity. However, in the short term, our efficiencies actually went down. We had to go through a period of more than a year just working to create the right platform for others to use. What carried us through that dip was the steadfast vision we created through strategic planning. We wanted an organization where you did not have to start from scratch every time you had a project. We wanted the kind of organization that understood that knowledge is not power; sharing that knowledge is power. So despite the temporary slowdown, the master toolbox created a set of standards and unified the customer experience. That created clarity for anyone seeking to lead. We focused on increasing strategy for growth instead of recreating project implementation.

Joe's Book: The Art of Business

A master toolbox with standards and processes is a strong foundation for when your business is running smoothly, and it creates clarity for leadership and the team. But what happens when the unexpected occurs? A project is delayed or there is a change in the market, and suddenly the workflow you so carefully constructed is disrupted.

To deal with this issue at Counsilman-Hunsaker, we started several knowledge-transfer practices around the art of business. First, we started with Joe, my father. He'd learned so much over his years as a business leader and serial entrepreneur, not only about the technical side of running a business, but in dealing with common obstacles that block good business acumen from developing. He knew how to work around challenges that we would undoubtedly come across, and how to evade mistakes we'd be bound to repeat without studying the past.

To initiate the process of transferring knowledge, I asked him to write down all the things that kept him up at night throughout the twenty-five years he had led Counsilman-Hunsaker. We made it into a piece called Joe's Book, full of "things Joe would say." It was his wisdom, peppered with his many sayings and quips. We printed them out and hung them on the walls of our office. You can still find that wisdom on the walls there to this day.

Joe and Scot Hunsaker - 2006

One saying from Joe's Book that made visitors pause was Joe's advice on accounts receivable: "When a client does not pay, wait for a choke point. Then, choke." We would use these phrases as a way to talk about the wisdom of what Joe meant and to reinforce the legacy that was already present in the organization.

Another example of the insights in Joe's Book includes something that kept him up at night: the phenomenon of a "floating pool." There are situations where there is more groundwater under a pool than in the pool. Without accounting for hydrostatic pressure, it's possible for a concrete pool to actually pop out of the ground. It's a really bad day when you walk into a client's facility and you see a pool three feet above where it's supposed to be. You can see the pipes hanging out of the sides, and the deck's pitched up. It's a nightmare. Because Dad wrote that down, the incoming leadership team had the opportunity to learn the physics of what caused it to happen. The positive effects didn't stop there. He was also imparting knowledge about how to deal with a situation like that, how to best interact with that customer, and how to fix it. His words taught both the science and the art of the business.

It is paramount that a leadership team be made aware of those steps, and that they understand it is not the end of the world when these things happen. It certainly isn't ideal, but you can recover from catastrophe. Further, it's how you attempt to recover in those moments that really sharpens and creates your business acumen.

All of this would be academic and useless if creating a legacy was not of the greatest importance. Joe could have kept this knowledge to himself, and, when he left the company, the knowledge would leave with him. There is no simple math that can reveal the value of the information he presented to us. To this day, Joe's Book—the physical one—still lives at Counsilman-Hunsaker. The collective wisdom of so many experiences is critical to successful legacy creation.

The Power of the Network

What is more important: what you know or who you know? One of the biggest barriers that new leaders face is not a lack of knowledge of how to do business, but a lack of an influential network.

As a business owner, you likely have a digital Rolodex of people who you can count on, and there is power in that. When you run into a challenge that seems insurmountable, you have a network that can help you. It is likely you have been of service to your network, as well.

At Counsilman-Hunsaker, we realized that if we wanted our new emerging leaders to be successful, then we needed to expand their knowledge and their networks. Meeting the right person is a jumpstart into the business world for emerging leaders. We wanted to do more than casual or random email introductions. We wanted our network to be visible to everyone in the organization and for the introductions to take place in a way that honored our relationships.

We decided one of the most effective ways to expose the leadership team to new resources and networks was "lunch and learn" events. We would call upon that network—be they vendors, leaders, colleagues, or thinkers—to share their knowledge with our team. This not only made powerful introductions, but it also was an opportunity to learn something new in our industry or about business in general. During my time at Counsilman-Hunsaker, we had over 1,500 lunch-and-learn events.

As valuable as this was, what we found even more valuable was the ability to archive that knowledge and call upon it when it was most critical. Each lunch-and-learn entry had a PowerPoint presentation, a bibliography of resources, and a bio of the speaker. A full audio file was also available in case a team member had to miss the lunch.

While this may seem like overkill or even a bit dubious, think of the business value of a database with thousands of searchable insights from industry leaders. Think of the confidence that the leadership team can have to make decisions when they know they are armed with more knowledge than anyone else in the industry. They became unstoppable.

I can't say it enough: the worst place you can store business information is in your head. Worse, if it exists only in your head and nowhere else, you haven't really stored it. You've time-stamped it with a finite expiration date. So, how do you get it out of your head and into the organization where it can continue your legacy? You record those ideas and experiences in a tangible, useful way. Every instinct you have may cry out against this, but it is critical to a real legacy.

Knowledge Is Power, but Only If You Share It

Tara ran headlong into this institutional-knowledge challenge when she was facing the prospect of creating a master toolbox. We began to take an inventory of her every business location and created the beginning of a best-practices platform for each management team. We also created an education program for new emerging leaders based on the tribal knowledge Tara had gathered over the years. Instead of starting from zero, each new leader received a jumpstart into the art of business.

Already, after only eighteen months, the company is beginning to see an increase in efficiencies. They suffered no setbacks after those handpicked leaders opted out of the strategic planning process. If anything, they are much more capable and agile as an organization. They are accomplishing more with fewer people.

Tara also has started to change her tune regarding her desires for legacy. No longer is she solely focused on selling to a third party. The process of sharing her knowledge and intentionally creating a legacy for her company has opened up options for her, and she is currently gearing up for her third round of strategic planning with a hungry, energized team of leaders.

The challenge for her will be what comes next in the process of creating a legacy: allowing your new leadership team to innovate upon the knowledge you have shared.

ACTION PLAN

- ✓ Work with your leadership team to create a plan that captures your repeatable business processes. This may look different for you than it did for me, but the point is that you are working against the starting-from-scratch mentality.
- ✓ Call upon your network to share their resources and insights with your team. You can create a process for capturing that knowledge, as well—one that is archival and digital.
- ✓ Encourage and reward the sharing of knowledge between departments and among your team. Recognize team members in your organization for their willingness to share knowledge.

CHAPTER 9

BE AN INNOVATOR,
NOT A GUARDIAN

KEY TAKEAWAYS

- ✓ Leaders manage change. If it were not for change, we would not need leadership.
- ✓ Create ways that people in the organization can make changes at the system level.
- ✓ Your legacy is more than a set of processes; it is a mindset.

I would like to give you permission to do something that you have always wanted to do. It's easy to accomplish, granted that you are not too terribly risk averse. I want you to not go into work tomorrow. Tell your team you're not available. Shut off your email, your text, your phone—everything. No connection to work. Just you and this book.

How do you think your team would do? If it were just one day, maybe it would not be so bad. This is assuming, of course, that you have done a good job at having authentic conversations, creating a leadership team, and equipping them with knowledge. I suspect they could be fine on their own. They may even be able to go for months. Essentially, they would be all set as long as one thing happened: everything always stayed the same.

We know, however, that this is never the case. In business things change all the time. The degree to which your team can adapt to change is the measure of their leadership. For a lot of business owners, there exists a need to control processes and the transfer of knowledge. This is natural. After all, the insights you have gathered usually came from experience, a code word for pain. But if you hope to create a legacy for your business, you must also confront the fact that each piece of knowledge you pass on has a born-on date. You must create a leadership team that can manage change. That is why the next step in creating your legacy is encouraging your team to look for ways to be innovators rather than custodians of knowledge.

Orchestrating a Comeback Based on Constant Improvement

For inspiration on creating a leadership team ready for change, I want to first introduce you to the father of change process. To do that, we need to travel to post-WWII Japan . . . not a thriving place. At the time, the country was severely depressed on every level, including economically. Conventional wisdom and the best knowledge we had said that it would take generation upon generation for the country to bounce back.

When most people saw a place that was void of any viable opportunities, W. Edwards Deming, American engineer and management consultant, saw a country poised for change. Deming is largely credited with helping to orchestrate the unlikeliest national comeback: the Japanese post-war economic miracle. His work began in 1950 in Tokyo, where Deming delivered a keynote address in which he outlined his philosophies: better design of products to improve service; higher level of uniform product quality; improvement of product testing in the workplace and in research centers; greater sales through global markets.

Shortly after this address, he applied his management theories to the Japanese manufacturers, including those in automobile production. He taught them to manage systems instead of managing people, a concept that was revolutionary at the time. "The system that people work in and the interaction with people may account for ninety or ninety-five percent of performance," said Deming.

In addition to being responsible for the turnaround of the post-WWII Japanese economy, I can testify that Deming is also partially responsible for inspiring change readiness in a privately held aquatics engineering firm in St. Louis during the early 2000s. While not nearly as noteworthy, it was a big deal to us.

By that time at Counsilman-Hunsaker, we had established a company dashboard, and we knew how to have authentic conversations. We also had started facilitating our strategic planning process and finding people who had the will and ability to lead. There were also systems in place to capture knowledge—both the science and the art of business. What we needed next was a way to mine opportunities to make improvements. We needed to go further if we hoped to a create a sustainable legacy. The question was: How could we synthesize a process for thinking critically about the systems we were using?

It was around that time that I was introduced to Deming's story and his methodologies for managing change. He had a knack for cutting right to the heart of management: "It is not necessary to change. Survival is not mandatory." In addition to his pithy insights, the consulting work he did in the '80s with Vernay Laboratories, an Ohio-based rubber manufacturer, gained him notoriety. He introduced them to a process he called the "Workers on the Red Beads." It inspired major changes and production improvements in the organization. When I introduced the process to my team, they looked at me a bit sideways. How would a game played with marbles shake loose where process improvements could be made?

It turns out the game allowed us to *perform* systemic change instead of *talk* about innovation. And we received more than just innovation ideas. The process created a path to leadership for key employees. It drove home that what we do as leaders is manage change. Culturally, it fit almost perfectly into some of the other practices we had already developed.

Creating a Culture of Innovation

Innovation is a buzzword within company cultures. Much in the same way that honesty or transparency is thrown around during business seminars, innovation has become a popular concept. The challenge, however, is how to knit innovation into the way you do business and to what end and for what purpose. Innovation for the sake of change is useless activity, but innovation in the context of creating a legacy is powerful.

It could be that you have a similar kind of stated commitment within your company to innovation. Here is a scenario for you: Let's say that someone approaches you with a new idea, and it's a good one. You express your enthusiasm for the idea to your employee. But ninety days later, nothing happens. Then the same person comes to you with another idea. This one is even better. "That's a great idea," you tell them. Then ninety days go by. Still, nothing happens. How likely do you think it is that you will get yet more ideas from this person? You know the answer. You won't.

As a way to create a culture of incremental improvements, we developed a *System Improvement Process* at Counsilman-Hunsaker. If a team lead or a person on the front line of the organization had an idea, we made a commitment to put their ideas to the test through this process.

Once the floodgates were opened and the people in our organization knew that their insights could shape the company, the ideas came in. These new ideas ranged from internal workflow-process improvements to investigating new customer audiences.

While I was CEO, our people brought forward over 3,200 system improvements. Not all of them worked, and some I did not like initially became a part of the maser toolbox. But that is the beauty of it. They were ideas that the leadership by itself would not have considered.

To be clear, my main goal was not to build a better toolbox. Sure, that was a great benefit, but the real purpose was to provide a structure on which people could innovate, and that we would have documentation of that process. I wanted to teach people how to manage change and lead even when things are uncertain or when they see the need for change.

How the System Improvement Process Works

Step One: The Situation Report. The first step in the System Improvement Process was the creation of a Situation Report. In almost every organization, when a mistake is made, there is a lot of energy spent complaining about the past. Complaining well becomes an art form for some people. As opposed to dwelling on mistakes or blaming people, we used these reports. Also, we wanted everyone to know that they were being paid to think and not merely to do what they were told. This structure allows for the exercise of leadership thinking: dealing with change and welcoming it as a sign of the need for improvement.

Step Two: Is this a real issue? Within the first thirty days of a new Situation Report, the leadership team would review. We would ask ourselves, "Do we have enough information to make a knowledgeable decision about how this needs to be handled?" It was rare that we did. So we would send our questions back to our team member and ask for more information.

Step Three: Change the toolbox? The team member would have thirty days to report back with more background or present research that would answer the questions. If they could not find more information or did not make the deadline, then the process was halted. If they presented more information to the leadership team, then we would review it once more. If we were satisfied with the ideas presented, then we would make a change to the toolbox. If we were not, then no change would be made.

This process—and the thinking behind it—is still in place at Counsilman-Hunsaker today. Recently, I spoke with a member of the leadership team at Counsilman-Hunsaker who is developing the process of gathering situation reports into an app. Not only does that exemplify how to innovate with institutional knowledge, it shows how your leadership team can innovate in ways you might not have imagined on your own. That's the key for leadership and the key to creating legacy: effectively managing change.

If you can encourage your team through creating structures for innovation, then you can essentially work yourself out of your job. You will have taught them to not just perform their function, but also to think, to know how to make changes. The results were profound. When I first purchased Counsilman-Hunsaker, I was probably doing 85 percent of the system improvements. By the time I sold the company, I had not done a Situation Report in at least three years. Who owned the business knowledge of Counsilman-Hunsaker in the early 2000s? I did. Who owned the intellectual property of Counsilman-Hunsaker in the last three years? *We* did. That reality set the stage for a path to actual ownership.

There are mountains of books on process improvement and management. The idea here was not so much the plan; it was the planning. We wanted people to know their ideas were more important than the machine we were building, and this system improvement process was just our way into that. Within your organization, the challenge is to teach people to do innovative work—to have a mindset more like an entrepreneur. The legacy that was important to me was the mindset and process it takes to manage change.

Uncovering Latent Leadership and Innovation

The theme I hope is emerging for you as you read this chapter has to do with why a culture of tangible innovation is critical to shaping your legacy. It was this insight around the need to create a mindset of constant systemic improvement that led us to Deming's Red Bead Game.

The idea behind the Red Bead Game is that you begin to notice where there are flaws in a system, not flaws with people. My leadership team would play this game at the end of successful projects. When we gathered to celebrate, we would have a dish full of beads, some white and some red. The white beads represented good things we experienced, and the red beads were challenges. Each player drew the same number of beads from the dish and gave an impromptu list of what we accomplished (for each white bead) and what could be improved (for each red bead). Another person helped to act as an archivist, cataloguing the data. What you end up with is a list of systems-based reviews from the people who were on the frontline of a project. We stored the beads in big jars and displayed them in our conference room as an artifact of what we had done together, both the good and the bad.

Often we would have vendors or even competitors in our space, and they would see our jars of beads. "What's that all about?" they would ask. Then I had the opportunity to explain our system improvement process and how much we were dedicated to those improvements, especially on projects that were successful. I received a lot of raised eyebrows. The tangible nature of this exercise provided windows to construct the narratives about what mattered most to our company. It was commitment that we could all see.

To be honest, I had expected that we would learn new ways to incrementally improve our processes. What I did not expect was the affect that a game like this would have on the leadership mindset of our company.

Macy, the receptionist turned business owner you read about in the last chapter, grabbed hold of the concepts in Deming's work faster than anyone else in the organization. As a result, she emerged as the best person to lead the celebrations and other occasions when we would use the game. The entire company started to see her as a natural leader with the organization. She was someone dedicated to being an innovator, not a custodian. Macy led by example. That meant when she became part of the strategic planning team, the transition seemed organic to everyone.

As I have said in previous portions of the book, there is no magic to any one of these practices taken separately. What matters most is why. You must allow for your desire to create a legacy to drive the execution of your action plan. This simple game and other practices created an environment for a certain kind of leadership to emerge. It was the kind of leadership that was ready for real company ownership.

ACTION PLAN

- ✓ Create a way to formalize incremental innovations within your company.
- ✓ Empower your whole organization to contribute change ideas to improve your processes. This requires the creation of a platform.
- ✓ Update your processes as new innovations come to light. Make certain these innovations are archived within the platform.

CHAPTER 10

TRUST WITH CONFIDENCE

KEY TAKEAWAYS

- ✓ You cannot trust with confidence until you have authentic conversations, emergent leadership, transfer of knowledge, and innovation culture.
- ✓ Trusting means that there is a deep understanding of what ownership really means.
- ✓ Setting up your business legacy requires you to have a clear definition of success and the plan to get there.

Partnerships don't work. At least, that's conventional business wisdom. According to multiple consulting firms, bankers, and attorneys, the failure rate for partnerships is just over 80 percent.[1] The trying experiences of many would have you convinced that ownership is best left to one person.

Those were facts that were not lost on Doug, Scott, and me. Back in 2002, when we decided to become partners in Counsilman-Hunsaker, we had seen partnerships go badly. But what was more important to us was the idea that we created a real model for ownership, something where everyone had skin in the game. But just what would our model look like? And how would we guard against the pitfalls that so many had experienced?

On a late Tuesday afternoon, Doug, Scott, and I sat down in my office to solve just that. We decided to start with the hard questions, ones that would get at the heart of what we meant when we said "ownership." The mistake that so many had made, it seemed to us, was not going right at the tough topics. We had every confidence that we could tackle them head on, because we had already accomplished so much together.

Since we had already had authentic conversations, we were used to looking at things from the same side of the table. Since we had created a planning process, new leaders had emerged. We had started to transfer business knowledge and encouraged everyone in the organization to innovate that knowledge. Thus, we were ready to trust with confidence and create a place for real ownership. And that is the final piece—the payoff—of creating a lasting legacy.

Trust, in this context, means something very specific. Most business owners think trusting their employees means knowing they'll do what they're told. But trusting with confidence means believing your leadership team can manage change and face an uncertain future. For legacy to take shape, you must nurture and embrace a sense of ownership within your upcoming leaders.

---

[1] Neville, Amanda. "Why Partnership Is Harder Than Marriage." Forbes. March 22, 2013. https://www.forbes.com/sites/amandaneville/2013/03/01/why-partnership-is-harder-than-marriage/#1cf9af6e7ec9.

Defining Ownership

On that fateful Tuesday, Doug, Scott, and I went to it. We began asking each other tough questions: If one of us dies, could a spouse be an owner? If there is a breach of trust, how do we handle it? What

OWNERSHIP CONVERSATION QUESTIONS

IF AN OWNER DIES, CAN THEIR SPOUSE
PARTICIPATE IN COMPANY DECISIONS?

YES
Lifestyle ownership

NO
Active ownership

CAN A 10-PERCENT OWNER PREVENT A 90-PERCENT
OWNER FROM BRINGING IN A NEW PARTNER?

YES
Equality in ownership

NO
He who holds the gold
makes the rules

IF AN OWNER RUNS INTO LEGAL TROUBLE,
CAN THEY STILL BE AN OWNER?

YES
No-morality clause

NO
Morality clause

is the process by which we can make decisions if one of us is no longer capable of leading? The questions numbered up to two hundred. They were all important, because the way we answered them would shape the culture of ownership within the company.

These conversations took place over many days, weeks, and months, and we all wrestled with them at night, on weekends, and in idle, quiet moments. This was a tug-of-war. We were defining what was most important, and we wanted to create expectations before situations presented themselves.

While it was hard, it also was oddly natural to us. We were accustomed to looking forward, and we were motivated to create a path to leadership for anyone who would emerge with the will and ability. Most importantly, we knew we were shaping the legacy of Counsilman-Hunsaker.

After countless hours of debate, we settled on an agreement, a white paper we called "Ownership Expectations." We used this document as a basis for the cultural identifiers of what being an owner means at Counsilman-Hunsaker. This was a summary of our beliefs about how we wanted to build the organization, and how we wanted to treat each other as owners, when things were good and bad. Much of it landed on the conclusion that the expectations increase when you're an owner as time goes on, not decrease. Right or wrong, this is what we believed.

This was a watershed moment for us. We were now painting the path to leadership in black and white. And this is critical for you as well. Why? The leading cause for divorce in this country is not finances or extramarital affairs; it is "unmet expectations." It is years of small behaviors that lead to unhappiness and ultimately a lack of trust. The same is true within organizations. Forging a partnership with someone in business is not unlike a marriage. In some ways, it is more intimate just because of the time spent together and the lives that depend upon you. So, if you do not have a list of partnership expectations and a definition of ownership, then you do not have real partners. And it is likely you will be doomed to repeat the mistakes of so many.

We took our Ownership Expectations to our attorneys and outside counsel. They structured formal company-specific agreements based upon the expectations we had outlined. The result was a clear, thorough understanding of what each of us expected from each other, so no one had to guess. Embedding these conversations into our company culture and putting them on paper helped align our mission and made the underlying gears work much more effectively. Once we had that in place, we had the groundwork set for our future owners, and what the expectations would be of them.

What I discovered here is this: there is power is making an agreement that begins with the organization. A lot of business-partnership arrangements start with attorneys. I cannot urge you enough to begin with the leadership team. Allow for your priorities to shape the culture of ownership before the process becomes formalized. Part of trusting with confidence and leaving a lasting legacy is trusting that your team—together—has the ability to set the expectations for what leadership means. This decision proved to be a critical one for us, and the same can be true of your organization.

We were armed with a document that outlined clearly the expectations we had for ourselves and anyone else who would step up as an owner. We then set in motion the process of introducing real ownership to our emergent leaders.

The Path to Real Ownership

When we identified someone with the will and ability to lead, we'd sit down with them and talk about our ownership plan. We'd explain the purpose. Ownership, as we understood it, was not a get-rich-quick scheme or retirement plan. Rather, we'd share about our vision for the future of the organization. We let them know we were focused on creating a leadership team that could manage change. Commitment to a team and a vision like that is not a light one, we would explain. Coming aboard the leadership team is essentially a professional marriage. It wouldn't make sense for the prospective leader to pursue it further if they'd thought about leaving the company. We'd let them know of an opening on the strategic planning team and ask the prospect to sit in on meetings. They could then consider becoming a member. This would give them the possibility to positively impact the firm at a strategic level, not just at a tactical level.

After a year or two, if that individual was still excelling in leadership and showing enthusiasm to know more about ownership, we'd tell them about how we value the company, how stocks are bought and sold, how distributions happen, and the inner workings of ownership. At this point, we had not yet made an offer. We'd simply be sharing the ideologies outlined in the white paper and talking through everything. The reason we were painstaking in this phase was because it was important to us that each new owner know what would be expected and how much a commitment like this meant.

It was only after we had confronted our prospect with the truth about ownership and what it meant to our culture that we would make a more formal offer. That offer was a step in something that we called "The Path to Ownership Process." This process allowed us the opportunity to be authentic in what ownership meant on a financial, personal, and legal level. Here is how it would work:

Legal counsel. If we made it to this point with a prospective leadership team member, we'd hand over a stack of legal documents three inches thick. This was the legal version of our white paper. We'd also give them a check to hire a lawyer to help them interpret what it is they would be signing. They had to make a knowledgeable decision. At no point in the process did we want there to be surprises. To feel like empowered leaders, potential part-owners need to know exactly what the documents mean. We would also preemptively point out spots that most lawyers would and wouldn't find advisable, and explain why they were there. They were the same places that our attorneys identified. That is because those were the areas that were best for the company and not always advantageous to one individual. We were all for one, one for all—and that does not translate perfectly into the legal system. Typically, they'd come back a few months later and say something along the lines of, "You're right. The lawyer loved this part and hated that one, but I understand why."

Stepping back a bit, let's examine the message all of this really sends. Do you think attaching a check to the legal documents helped address any level of sheer terror that the employee may be experiencing? Think about the message. Our job as leaders is to provide the opportunities for others to be comfortable being uncomfortable. It shows that you trust them to make the best decision possible with the tools at our disposal, and that's what it would be like for them to work with you on the leadership team. It builds trust and develops their confidence in the whole process.

Compensation. Here is something that most people don't know about being an owner: you get paid last. As one of my clients once astutely pointed out, there is a big difference between signing the back of the paycheck and signing the front of the paycheck. When you are an employee, you get paid every two weeks. When you are an owner, you get to figure out what you need to do so everyone has a paycheck in two weeks. Being an owner means that you have a responsibility not just for your employees, but all their families, as well. It's a big change.

The Path to Ownership Process that we had at Counsilman-Hunsaker gave us the ability to talk about cash flow—how to manage money personally and for the company. I have witnessed poor cash-flow management destroy more companies than anything else.

This Path to Ownership Process is an entry point into how we talk about sharing the profits and rewards of working together—that we all succeed and fail together. There are other aspects of ownership that are just not discussed in most business-school programs. They fall into the school of hard knocks, and they are the kinds of issues we dealt with in our Path to Ownership Process.

Equity presentation. Another example of the kind of lessons we taught through how we presented equity to our new owners had to do with equity within the company. They had to purchase it themselves. We did not give the stock of the company away, and we did not lend the money to purchase stock to our new owners. Instead, we wanted them to get used to establishing a relationship with a bank.

There are a number of sound business reasons for why new owners should get to know a bank, and all of them are helpful. But the reasons that we had the banking model as part of our Path to Ownership Process was to get at the tougher side of ownership. The bank is not only going to make the new owner sign the loan and present personal financial statements, but they're going to make the spouse sign the loan, as well. The part of being an owner that no one tells you about is how many nights you will be up worrying about money with your spouse and how you are going to make payments.

Future leaders must understand that private business ownership is an all-in family proposition. It is a commitment not just for the leader, but for the spouse. Making decisions like this one has the potential to create tension in one's home life if not handled transparently. Shared fate gave us the understanding and the structure to allow families of owners to learn what ownership really means.

And since we were all for one, one for all, they could learn from the mistakes the previous owners had made.

Trust Is Not Compliance

I hope you get the chance to experience the kind of trust that I did. It is the culmination of a commitment to a legacy-building model for leadership. That kind of trust is something most people do not get to experience.

Trust does not mean compliance. It does not mean potential leaders must do what they're told. Not only are attempts to control people futile; they alienate the very leadership talent that makes this process work. This is not about following orders. It is about having the confidence to know that you've selected people who have the willingness and ability to lead, and that they'll be able to manage the change required for a successful future. It is knowing they have your back.

If you have authentic conversations, create an engaging culture, transfer knowledge, and encourage employees to run with it, then you've established a foundation of trust amidst your leaders. This kind of trust isn't based just on your gut instinct anymore. It's now grounded in something real. Even if it isn't your intention to sell or transfer your company to your employees, the aforementioned steps will make your company much more effective. Also, an engaged leadership team makes your organization much more valuable to a third party. Going through this process gives you powerful options and choices for whatever you may face, which you'll have the privilege of confronting with your team.

No matter what lies ahead for you, I urge you to make a real beginning. Find what is most exciting to you and create the action plan necessary to get there. If you have made it through this book, you have everything you need. Begin your legacy plan now—not just for yourself, but because your team needs you. We need your leadership and knowledge to shape the health and foundations of our economy and our well-being. With the full knowledge of what is at stake for your company, make a vision and plan to get there. You can join with those of us who have come before and create something that will live on long after you are gone.

A Cautionary Tale

Doug is a personal friend and colleague from my days at Counsilman-Hunsaker. Over thirty years ago, he founded an engineering company. At the time, they were the young, up-and-coming mover and shaker in the industry. That original team was tight knit and dynamic. They managed to grow and create success with their ingenuity. That said, Doug was the authoritative leader. Everyone followed his vision for the company, and he played the role of benevolent dictator with ease.

Months ago, I received a call from Doug. Now in his late seventies, he was starting to see that he had to find a way to exit the company. He knew his days were numbered. He thought that I could facilitate the same kind of process that led to the sale of Counsilman-Hunsaker.

We met on several occasions over the following months. Within Doug's company, there were two camps: the old guard versus the new generation. And those two camps had been at war with each other for years. We started to implement authentic conversations, hoping this would create the platform for deeper discussion. But getting everyone to the same side of the table proved tenuous. In every attempt to look in the same direction, we quickly ran into a trust barrier. Unfortunately, it was simply too high to overcome.

Still not willing to give up, we discovered a handful of people who emerged as leaders through some planning processes. However, that old guard—the group that had been there since the founding—would not let go of the "command and control" model they had seen from Doug.

What happened next is perhaps the saddest of outcomes. People began to leave. With no path to leadership and no way to overcome the lack of trust, Doug's company contracted. A lifetime worth of business-building knowledge went away, and with it, the livelihoods of fifty employees and their families.

I tell you this story because what was missing from Doug's company was not intelligence or drive. He certainly did not lack a desire to serve his employees. Indeed, he cared a great deal for them. What he lacked was the fundamental understanding of what a legacy

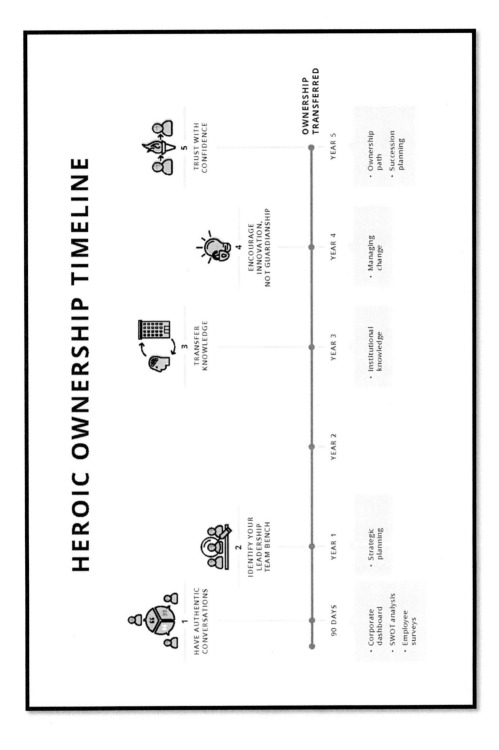

really is. What I have offered you is a path. But if you wait, even for a moment, to begin creating your legacy, you are risking your chance at creating the kind of legacy that will fit your definition of success. Quite simply, you are mortal. You will run out of time to make the impact you hope to have.

Doug missed perhaps the most important point of all: everything you do creates a legacy. It is not created in the last year of ownership. It is created continuously. You are, in this moment, setting the course for your company. It is incumbent upon you to avoid the same mistakes of so many business leaders. You must create your plan and begin now. The happiness and livelihood of so many, including those closest to you, hangs in the balance.

ACTION PLAN

✓ Define ownership. Make your culture lead your path to ownership.

✓ Create a path to test new leaders. Be transparent in what is expected.

✓ Test the process with your leadership team.

EPILOGUE

MOMENT OF TRUTH

For some people, creating a legacy means having their name on a building or achieving financial success. Maybe it means achieving fame and fortune or never being forgotten.

For me, creating a legacy is knowing that there are generations of people who are going to be impacted by the kinds of leadership we developed with my partners and employees at the company we built. It's knowing that there will be a lasting culture of trust in others and a real sense that the work is meaningful long after I'm gone. The work is meaningful not only to me, but to our team members and their families, my family, and to the generations of people to whom we'll pass the torch. That's what we did, and it'll keep happening because we'll have taught subsequent generations how. If we can move the needle on building these practices into the business world, then to me, we've created a legacy. It's knowing that your legacy is being shaped in the present moment, then taking actions that reflect that belief.

After having reviewed the tools outlined in this book, perhaps you can now see why the day I sold Counsilman-Hunsaker to my employees was so significant. To me, it was that very definition of legacy. It was passing along what we had built to the next set of leaders, thereby setting the cycle of positive, impactful leadership in motion. That day was representative of the culture we'd built at the company and the lessons that I hoped were passed along to other leaders.

It was October 2012 when two of my partners came to me, essentially asking to buy Counsilman-Hunsaker from me. Further, they communicated that most 1 and 2–percent company owners wanted a larger portion, and came to them asking how that could happen. This was coming from a group of people who had been at the company for around five years and never expected to be business owners. But once they had been initiated into our culture, learned who we were through authentic conversations, and learned how to effectively deliver our value proposition, they had the passion and drive to take the company into the future. They were ready to push all their chips in and risk their own financial futures on the company. That level of commitment and willingness was a testimony to the character and confidence we had developed over the years.

I then asked my partners if they had financing, and, of course, they did. The bank they had utilized was one that we had worked with for twelve years at the company. The bankers understood them and the culture of our company. The bank also believed in the leadership team's will and ability to lead, which created a sense of confidence in the transaction from both sides.

We completed the deal in very short order. I never believe in making a business decision solely on tax policy, but the capital-gains tax was going to change in forty-five days. So, I said, "I'm willing to leave a little money on the table, but I'm not willing to do it twice. If we're going to do this, we're going to do it in forty-five days." And we did.

Exactly forty-five days later, I sold 100 percent of my outstanding stock to my team members for cash. I believe there's no way that could have happened if we hadn't built a leadership team, and if we hadn't worked on all of the phases described in this book leading up to letting go and trusting with confidence in what we had built. We had already created an understanding between us; we weren't starting from scratch. We were doing the same transaction we had already done so many other times, except this time, the numbers just happened to be a lot bigger.

I could not help but think of Joe, my father. And I could not think of a better tribute to his character than what I saw around me at that table. Though we differed on our ideas of leadership and management, his intention to create something that was long-lasting was a drive I could feel. That feeling was not lost on me. It added another layer of meaning to an already momentous day.

None of this would have happened if the other owners around the table did not understand what all of this meant. They would not have risked their personal financial futures for themselves and for their families without the confidence and capacity we mutually created.

Your legacy, that thing you will leave behind, hinges on your ability to execute the five steps outlined in this book. It is your job as the leader to create a leadership team that can make knowledgeable decisions about business. And your journey has already started—it's not too late to take a new direction if your company deserves better.

THE LEADERSHIP BENCH SPEAKS

INSIGHTS FROM OTHERS AT COUNSILMAN-HUNSAKER

Nothing of great importance or impact happens in a vacuum. There is that old adage usually attributed to coaching legend John Wooden: "It is amazing what happens when no one gets the credit." The same has been true of the events that I can point to in my life and call a success.

This is why I believe that the voices and insights of the leadership team we assembled at Counsilman-Hunsaker would be helpful to round out your understanding of what creating a legacy is really like.

Throughout this book, you saw the pronoun "we" appear many times. That is because it was a "we" effort. The following are the characters and personalities that make up that "we."

One thing in general that nearly everyone said was that they would not change a thing; they would do it over again.

December 12, 2012: Closing with the Counsilman-Hunsaker Leadership Team

This was most encouraging because, as you likely could imagine, creating a leadership culture was tough. But, in the end, most everyone felt it was worth it.

As part of this section, I have included those who did not remain with the company after it transitioned to the next generation of the leadership team. I did this for two reasons: One is that it is living up to the authentic conversations that we had. And, two, I think their insights are equally valuable. In business and in the creation of a legacy, there are outcomes that we will not foresee.

Here are some of the insights and takeaways (the good and the bad) gathered from the team.

A Proven Path to Leadership Increases Confidence

"My first impression was that I could tell the company knew what they were doing. Over time, that is an impression that I have had confirmed from other people in other industries and businesses. The pace was something that took some getting used to. It is a lot to learn quickly, and you have to take some initiative. But because I have now done it and lived it, I would not offer a change."

—Kevin Post, Owner, Principal, Counsilman-Hunsaker

"From the start, I could see that there was an identifiable plan for how company leadership worked and how decisions were made. The sharing of business knowledge creates a level of trust. Honestly, the plan to transition ownership was what brought me to Counsilman-Hunsaker. It piqued my interest. I could see that I had the ability to move forward."

—Jeff Nodorft, Owner, Principal, Counsilman-Hunsaker

Sharing Financials and Transparency Changes the Conversation

"Looking back, I think our decision to share finances was a pivotal moment. It worked well to have the dashboard, and we still rely on it. I am amazed that other organizations do not have that dashboard. Professionals are not always the best people when it comes to how to interpret numbers, so the financial dashboard is a strong key in creating a different conversation."

—Scott Hester, Owner, President, Counsilman-Hunsaker

"It was good to feel like a part of a team. The openness and the flow of information was not something I was used to, and sharing what we were doing financially was a wonderful experience. It gave me the ability to share in the process."

—Andy Crippen, Project Manager, Westport Pools

"The transparency regarding the state of the business worked well. I remember that we spent a lot of time with the family meetings, and everyone was feeling like a part of the organization. We celebrated successes, and when things were not going well, everyone knew."

—Steve Crocker, Director of Sport Swimming, Water Technology Inc.

Investing in the People (and Not the Machine) Allows for Emerging Leadership

"From the get-go, it was a very empowering culture. We are committed to giving people the tools they need, getting them in the right seat on the bus, and getting out of the way. Others in our industry do not take that approach. They are slower to offer leadership and development opportunities. We were put in situations for accelerated growth. I remember being supported in hosting speaking engagements, and I was encouraged to enhance my profile in the industry and with the industry associations. Still today, we invest in everyone's development and introduce study groups to round out each individual."

—Carl Nylander, Owner, Principal, Counsilman-Hunsaker

"The strategic planning process as a path to leadership was a homerun for us. It gave the opportunity for voices to be heard. And that is how you get buy-in from others in the organization and find new leaders."

—Scott Hester, Owner, President, Counsilman-Hunsaker

Advice: Start Planning Legacy Immediately to Avoid Bad Decision-Making

"I would recommend the journey to real ownership as a leadership process for any business. It sets the transition in motion long before it becomes critical. I have been in organizations where there was no preplanning. So as time goes on, the potential for transfer becomes more and more desperate. That desperation leads to worse and worse decisions. Then there can be a lack of trust for good information. At Counsilman-Hunsaker, the planning is done ahead of time, before it becomes a necessity. If you are rushed into an ownership transition, you are looking to get out, so you may misidentify who should be in charge."

—Jeff Nodorft, Owner, Principal, Counsilman-Hunsaker

Leadership Focus Makes It Hard to Keep Middle Management

"When you have ownership opportunities and a leadership culture, it is hard to keep people in the middle. The culture we created makes for a lot of momentum. It means a lot of chefs and not a lot of cooks. And we could use more cooks. With this system, it is challenging to keep people in the middle, because that leaves them feeling like they are on the outside looking in."

—Keven Post, Owner, Principal, Counsilman-Hunsaker

"We are good at creating structure, but the implementation is a struggle. Some pieces move forward and others do not. It is a challenge to identify and reinforce what is important across all of the departments as we grow. And when certain pieces do not move at the same pace, it creates less consistency and accountability. We continue to challenge ourselves to make our aspirations match reality."

—Jeff Nodorft, Owner, Principal, Counsilman-Hunsaker

APPENDIX

TURNING YOUR EMPLOYEES INTO OWNERS

Scot Hunsaker

About Scot Hunsaker

Scot Hunsaker is the former CEO of Counsilman-Hunsaker, where he grew the company's revenue by a factor of ten, quadrupled the employees, and opened four new offices in North America. He sold the firm to his employees for cash in 2012.

Scot now runs the Ardent Group, whose mission is to help business owners prepare for a healthy succession by teaching their employees how to think like owners.

ARDENT

314.283.1589

scot@ardentgroup.com
www.ardentgroup.com

...ercent of companies fold when current leadership leaves.

Are you one of them? "

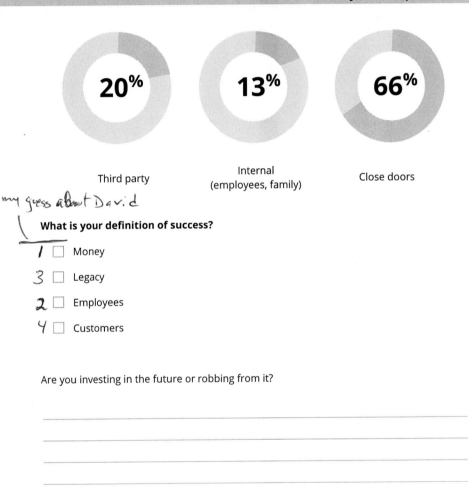

Third party

Internal
(employees, family)

Close doors

my guess about David

What is your definition of success?

1 ☐ Money

3 ☐ Legacy

2 ☐ Employees

4 ☐ Customers

Are you investing in the future or robbing from it?

_____

_____

_____

_____

_____

Ardent Group

Step 1: Authentic Conversations

Corporate Dashboard

What tools do you use to see into the future?

_____

_____

What tools do you want to add to your dashboard?

_____

_____

How can you more effectively share your information?

_____

_____

Considerations:

- ✓ Trailing twelve-month averages: _Up is good; down is bad._
- ✓ Quoting, new contracts, revenue, backlog

Ardent Group

95

SWOT Analysis

Our Hits — What were our successes in the last year? Our home runs? What went right?

Our Misses — What went wrong in the last year? What did we shoot for, but missed?

Our Strengths — Where's our horsepower that makes us a great company?

Our Weaknesses — What imperfections hold us back from being even greater?

Our Opportunities — What favorable possibilities are on the horizon (internal and external)?

Our Threats — What potholes lie in the road ahead that could destroy our good efforts?

President for a Day — If you could be president for one day, one decision, what would it be?

One Thing — What one thing could the company change to make you more effective?

Employee Surveys

Conduct these annually, share them with your team, and track multiple years of data.

Survey Topics

- ✓ Leadership
- ✓ Mission and values
- ✓ Governance and accountability
- ✓ High-performance work
- ✓ Working environment
- ✓ Trust
- ✓ Employee engagement
- ✓ Satisfaction
- ✓ Development
- ✓ Legal and ethics

Customer Surveys

Conduct these annually, share them with stakeholders, and use them as a marketing tool.

Kitchen Cabinet

Step 2: Engagement

Bench Strength

Who has the will and ability to lead?

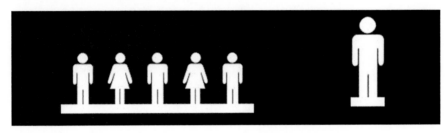

How have they demonstrated their will and ability to lead?

How can they demonstrate their will and ability to lead?

Don't set up for failure!

- ✓ Three strikes (accountability)
- ✓ Infant mortality
- ✓ *Who Says Elephants Can't Dance?* by Lou Gerstner, IBM
- ✓ Share with Vistage group

Step 3: Transferring Knowledge

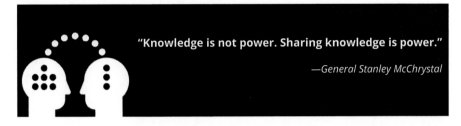

"Knowledge is not power. Sharing knowledge is power."

—General Stanley McChrystal

How do you get institutional knowledge out of individuals' heads and into the organization?

What other tools can you use to capture and transfer institutional knowledge?

Considerations:

- ✓ Master toolbox: Production, marketing, accounting, human resources, education
- ✓ Joe's Book: What keeps you up at night?
- ✓ For what it is worth: Legacy culture of leader/owner
- ✓ Lunch and learns: Capture the knowledge

—Vendor coming in ⟨ fill out speaker summary
- share PPT (softcopy)
- agree to be filmed + recorded
• put on server/organize

Ardent Group

Step 4: Teach Innovation, Not Custody

How do you teach the ability to manage change?

System Solution Process

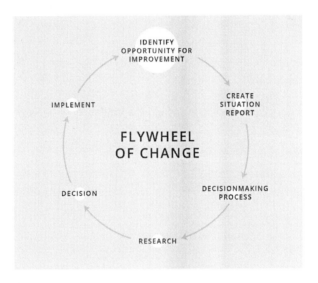

Considerations:

- ✓ Red beads, situation report, knowledge base, celebration
- ✓ What issue would you not let go more than ninety days?

Ardent Group

Step 5: Trusting with Confidence

Learn how to be comfortable being *uncomfortable*.

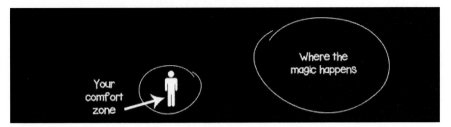

Shared Fate

Create common definition of success

- ✓ One for all, all for one
- ✓ Paid monthly, paid by check
- ✓ Hand them out personally

Create common definition of ownership

- ✓ Fifty questions: White paper summarizing expectations

Invitation process: Date for three years

Purpose lunch: Demonstrate will and ability to lead

Detail lunch: Circle of life, legal counsel

Ardent Group

Key Takeaways

Your legacy starts today!

How are you preparing for the future?

_____

_____

_____

_____

_____

_____

What is your definition of success?

_____

_____

_____

_____

_____

_____

Other Takeaways

- ✓ Having employees who think like owners provides you options for the future
- ✓ You can't turn your employees into owners; they have to do so themselves
- ✓ You can't do it yourself—you need the **POWER** of the **TEAM**

Ardent Group

ARDENT

SITUATION REPORT

TOPIC: [   ]   **DATE:** [   ]
                                        AUTHOR: [   ]

OBSERVATIONS:

_____
_____

OPTIONS:

_____
_____

RECOMMENDATIONS:

_____
_____

DECISION:

_____
_____

DATE APPROVED: [   ]   **BEAD COLOR:** ☐ Green ☐ White ☐ Red

KNOWLEDGE MANAGEMENT:

Check box if update to document is required and attach separate document with changes.

☐ Operations manual   ☐ Project workflow   ☐ Production manual
☐ Design criteria manual   ☐ Training material   ☐ Master specs
☐ Blog topic   ☐ Other: _____

Ardent Group

103

ABOUT THE AUTHOR

 Scot Hunsaker is the former CEO of Counsilman-Hunsaker, where he grew the company's revenue by a factor of ten, quadrupled the employees, and opened four new offices in North America. He sold the firm to his employees for cash in 2012.

Scot now runs the Ardent Group, whose mission is to help business owners prepare for a healthy succession and teach their employees how to think like owners.